THE ABC's OF MISSING "U"

"Comfort for the moments when words are hard to find— as you journey through grief, A to Z."

The ABC's of Missing "U"

"Comfort for the moments when words are hard to find—
as you journey through grief, A to Z."

Eran Poole

JAM Adventures Coaching and Publishing Agency

Copyright © 2025 Eran Poole
Published by JAM Adventures Coaching and Publishing Agency.
All rights reserved.

This book is a work of original authorship protected under U.S. Copyright Law and international copyright laws. No part of this publication may be reproduced, stored in a retrieval system, or transmitted in any form or by any means—electronic, mechanical, photocopying, recording, or otherwise—without the prior written permission of the publisher, except for brief quotations used in reviews or scholarly works. Unauthorized reproduction or distribution is prohibited and punishable by law.

ISBN: 979-8-9987582-0-1

Printed in the United States of America.

This book is dedicated to You.

You who are trying.
You who are holding on to your faith.
You who are still believing in God's plan.
You who keep showing up the best way you know how.
This book is for you—
You whose grief has just begun,
And you whose grief has lingered for as long as you can remember.
You who need a message.
You who need encouragement.
You who need a gentle reminder that you are deeply loved.
You who need the whisper that you are necessary.
To you who needs the validation that your feelings and emotions are real—and that they deserve the space you've created for them.
This book is for you—missing someone, or maybe many people.
May you never lose yourself to your grief.
I pray this book becomes the bridge that helps you remember:
Even in the midst of heartbreak, there are still beautiful things to stand on.

This book is dedicated to you—
Not just for your healing,
But to encourage your momentum.
You are still seen.
You are still heard.
You are still you.
Let's journey through this together.

You are my Inspiration

You inspire me to keep writing. Watching you experience what's new to me has inspired me to find ways I can help serve you in this journey. You have inspired me to pick my passion for writing back up. While my preferred writing style has shifted for this, you have inspired me to let God stretch me.

You have inspired me to hold on to my faith and hold on to my smile. I'm inspired to let my tears fall and to let my heart hurt in the many ways that it does—every single second of every single day. You have helped me remember that the plans God has for me are still beautiful and that His promises are still true.

You have inspired me to try again.

You have inspired me to finish what I've started.

You have inspired me to get back to the place of giving God control of my pen.

You have inspired me, even through my hurt, to keep finding ways to win. Even when I don't have the words—God does. He's still speaking. He's still listening. And He still loves YOU.

You've inspired me to show you that truth.

So thank you.

Introduction

Grief is heavy. It doesn't ask for permission, and it doesn't follow a schedule. One moment, life feels normal, and the next, everything has changed. It's messy, unpredictable, and exhausting. But if there's one thing I've learned, it's this: grief is not the end of your story.

For the past two and a half years, I have been learning—sometimes stumbling—through my own grief journey. In August 2023, I lost my best friend. Six months later, I lost my mother. Both were full of life, full of plans, and then, just like that, they were gone. Although I had experienced grief before, this time was different. This time, grief knocked the breath out of me. It silenced me, consumed me, and left me feeling defenseless. Losing my mother—the woman who raised me, guided me, and loved me without conditions—left me shattered in ways I never imagined.

I have spent the last year and a half walking through the fog of loss, searching for light, wondering how I would ever feel normal again. There were days I didn't know how to move forward, and other days I wasn't sure I wanted to. I have carried the weight of heartbreak, the lump in my throat that wouldn't go away, and the exhaustion of grief that makes even the smallest tasks feel impossible. But even in the middle of all of that, I have learned something I didn't expect: I am still here.

 I am not writing this from the other side of grief; I am writing this from inside of it.

This book started as a way to help my youngest brothers, nieces, and nephews understand what they were feeling. But as I wrote, I realized that I needed these affirmations just as much as they did. These are the words I wish someone had spoken over me. These are the reminders that I have had to hold on to for dear life. Writing this has stretched me, challenged me, and, in some ways, healed me. It has shown me that grief is not something you just "get over." It is something you learn to carry.

Grief is not a disease. It is not a curse. It is not something that means you are broken beyond repair. Grief is love searching for home. It is proof that you had something, someone, worth missing. It is the weight of love that still exists, even when the person is no longer physically here.

As a certified professional life coach, my desire is to meet people where they are and help them find a healthy way to cope with grief. That doesn't mean forcing understanding where there is none, but it does mean finding hope.

1 Thessalonians 4:13 (HCSB) reminds us, "We do not want you to be uninformed, brothers, concerning those who are asleep, so that you will not grieve like the rest, who have no hope."

We grieve, but we do not grieve like the world does—hopeless, lost, and defeated. We grieve with hope. Hope that God is still with us. Hope that love does not die. Hope that the people we have lost are not truly lost at all.

This is not a step-by-step guide to healing. This is not a book filled with clichés about how time will fix everything. This is a book for the moments when you don't have the words. It's for the days when grief feels like too much. It's for those of us who still believe that even in loss, there is life.

I want this book to remind you that grief is not the end of your story. I want to help you remember the joy, the love, and the memories that make the pain worth carrying. I want to encourage you to hold on to hope, even when it feels impossible.

You are not alone in this. Grief is hard, but we can walk through it together. And even in the middle of it, even when it feels impossible—you are still here. And that means there is still light ahead.

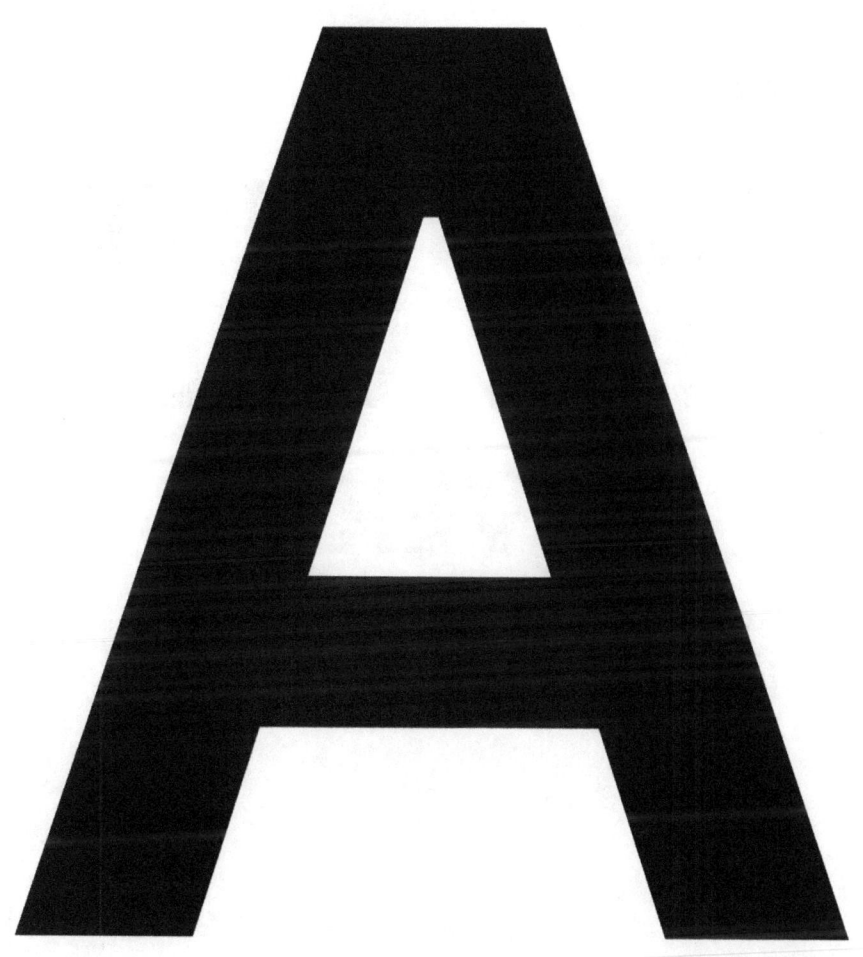

ALL THE LOVE THAT YOU'VE FELT, WILL NEVER BE FORGOTTEN.

Think about the things that remind you of how deeply that person loved you. It could be remembering how often they said, "I love you," the way their voice sounded when they spoke, or the small, thoughtful gestures they made that showed their love in ways words couldn't. Focus on these memories, allowing them to wrap around you like a comforting blanket.
Sometimes, it's enough to simply sit quietly and reflect on what being loved by them truly felt like—the safety, the warmth, the joy.

The intention here is not to dwell on the fact that they are no longer physically present to love you. Instead, it's to remind you that their love is something you can still feel. Love isn't tangible; it's a feeling where we pour our emotions to express our deepest gratitude, admiration, and care for someone. When someone passes away, their love doesn't leave. Love is what remains—it's what stays with you.

Take the time, as often as you need, to remind yourself not only of how much they loved you, but also how much you love them.

Dwelling on the fact that you are loved doesn't erase the pain that grief brings. It doesn't soften the blow of realizing that love is all you have left to hold on to. But it does serve as a gentle reminder that love is as big as you allow it to be. As big as it is, you can also make it as small and compact as you need to carry it with you every single day.

Grief and love often coexist in a delicate balance. While grief reminds you of what you've lost, love reminds you of what you'll always have. And as you navigate your journey through loss, let the love you shared be your anchor—a source of strength, comfort, and connection that will never fade.

I know it's hard, and I know this may not seem doable at all times, but you are capable of trying every single day. You're not alone in this, love. No matter how foggy the day may feel, and no matter how blurry the tears may make your eyes, allow love to be what weighs you down in all of this—not the burden of what is evidently missing. All the love you felt is still here with you.

This isn't about being strong. It's about the continuous attempt to keep trying to remember.

You are still loved. So loved. I know this all seems off balance, but you are still being carried.

I love you.

Scripture Reference: Romans 8:38-39 (HCSB)
"For I am persuaded that not even death or life, angels or rulers, things present or things to come, hostile powers, height or depth, or any other created thing will have the power to separate us from the love of God that is in Christ Jesus our Lord."

This passage is a reminder that nothing—not even death—can separate us from love. God's love is eternal, and so is the love we shared with those we've lost. Grief makes us feel like we are missing a part of ourselves, but love remains. Love is in the lessons they taught us, the memories we cherish, and the way their presence shaped our lives. When grief tries to convince us that loss is all we have left, this scripture reminds us that love never leaves. Just as God's love is constant, so is the love of those who have touched our lives.

Affirmation:

"Love never leaves. I carry the love of those I've lost in my heart every day. Their love is my strength, my comfort, and my reminder that I am still deeply cherished. I choose to focus on the love I still have, not just the loss I feel."

Final thought:

Grief may remind us of what we've lost, but love reminds us of what we will always have. Let love be what anchors you, brings you peace, and gives you hope, knowing that nothing—not even death—can separate us from love.

No matter your age, the truth remains the same—our loved ones are not lost, and neither are we. Heaven is a place of joy, love, and complete freedom. We can grieve, but we can also hold onto hope. Our journey isn't over yet, but when the time comes, we will be reunited in the most beautiful way. Keep living with purpose, because one day, we will all be home.

BELIEVE IN YOUR HEART THAT YOU WILL SEE THEM AGAIN ONE DAY.

As believers, we are taught that when a person passes away, we will see them again one day—when we all arrive in Heaven. Often, we associate Heaven with death, but we seldom equate it with freedom. One of the most comforting truths is that Heaven is a place free from pain, hurt, fear, and even the concept of death itself.

When God calls someone home, Heaven becomes their eternal home. Shifting your mindset to understand that a loved one has reached the absolute end of earthly life only to begin the most beautiful part of existence with Jesus can bring profound comfort. It serves as a reminder that each day we are striving to meet Jesus in Heaven and to live with Him forever.

Our loved ones now experience the rest and freedom that Heaven offers—a freedom that this world could never provide. It's a beautiful reminder to live each day with the purpose of reaching Heaven ourselves so that we can see them again. Imagine being reunited with the person you've lost, witnessing them bask in the one thing this world cannot give: complete and absolute freedom. That's the gift Heaven brings. When our loved ones pass away, we don't truly lose them. Through our tears, we can find joy in knowing they have gained access to the most beautiful place eternity has to offer.

And the best part? When we see them again, they'll be there to welcome us and guide us through Heaven like the best tour guides we could ever imagine.

You still have a purpose that you are called to fulfill. Losing someone can make you feel like nothing else matters—but that's a lie. Your purpose still matters. Your mission didn't die when your loved one passed away. Your journey to Heaven is still important. There is still a future and a hope for you!

I know what the give-up feels like. Each day, I strive to keep going. Why? Because I have a goal—to see my mother again. To laugh with my best friend again. I live to see Jesus.

Death has a way of robbing your memory of what you've been promised: everlasting life. Heaven is a promise we believe is ours. You cannot stop living. You must keep living. There is purpose in your living. Your existence is attached to purpose. One day, you'll be able to share the testimony of what "I kept going" means. "You'll see them again" is a promise. Keep going. And when that day comes for reuniting, be empty—because you kept pouring from your purpose.

I know what it feels like to be upset with God. Why continue to serve the One who let you hurt? Because His purpose is still tied to a plan. A plan that needs you. Believe in your heart that this still all works out for your good.

I love you.

Scripture: Revelation 21:4 (HCSB)
"He will wipe away every tear from their eyes. Death will no longer exist; grief, crying, and pain will exist no longer because the previous things have passed away."

Heaven is not just a destination—it is the fulfillment of God's promise to us. When we think about losing someone, our minds often focus on the pain of separation. However, this verse reminds us that Heaven is a place where pain, suffering, and death no longer exist. The hurt we feel here on earth will be completely erased in eternity. Our loved ones are not suffering anymore. They are experiencing a level of peace and joy that we can only imagine. This verse encourages us to shift our grief into hope, understanding that they are truly free and that we, too, will experience that freedom one day.

Affirmation:
"My loved one is not lost—they are free. They are in the presence of Jesus, experiencing a life without pain, sorrow, or death. I will hold onto the promise of Heaven and live with purpose, knowing I will see them again."

Final Thought:
Grief and hope can exist together. It's okay to mourn, but don't let grief overshadow the joy of knowing that your loved one has gained eternal peace. Let their journey to Heaven be a reminder to keep striving for your own heavenly home. Live each day with purpose, love deeply, and trust in God's promise of eternity.

CHERISH THE MEMORIES THAT YOU HAVE. THEY ARE YOURS TO HOLD ON TO FOREVER.

Your memories are not a form of torture. They are not there to harm you, but to remind you of the experiences you were blessed to have. Whether joyful or painful, your memories are uniquely yours—precious moments that remain etched in your heart forever. When a loved one passes away, the memories you've created together don't vanish. Instead, they become a bridge—a powerful connection that keeps their presence alive within you.

While you can no longer see, touch, or speak to them, your memories hold the ability to bring you close to them again. Through these recollections, you can revisit shared moments, relive their laughter, hear their voice, and feel their love. It's true that reflecting on memories can sometimes bring tears— tears of longing, because those moments are no longer within your reach. But within those tears lies a profound beauty: the acknowledgment of a love so significant, so meaningful, that it left an indelible mark on your soul.

Every memory is an imprint on your heart, a treasure you carry with you always. Even through grief, memories hold the power to bring comfort. They can make you smile at the thought of their humor, laugh at a shared joke, or feel safe remembering their embrace.

These memories remind you of the moments that defined your love for them and their love for you. They are not just fragments of the past but living gifts—experiences you can revisit time and time again. Each memory serves as a light in the darkness of loss, a reminder that the bond you shared was real, unbreakable, and enduring.

Memories also serve as a testament to the impact someone had on your life. They reflect not just who they were, but who they helped you become.

They are the evidence of a love so profound that it transcends physical absence, allowing their presence to linger in your heart.

So, when grief feels overwhelming, remember that your memories are not meant to cause pain but to preserve the essence of the one you've lost. They are there to celebrate the love you shared, to honor their life, and to remind you of the beauty that can still be found in the past, even as you navigate the future.

Your memories are a gift. Cherish them, lean into them, and allow them to be a source of solace as you continue to carry your loved one with you in spirit.

Don't let your memories taunt you. Sometimes, the weight of a memory can feel stiffening to the heart—because let's be honest: memories are not enough when you want that person here with you. It can feel taunting because they're all you have left.

Cry and be sad when you need to—this is certainly a struggle. But don't let the spirit of taunt overpower the power of your memories.

I encourage you to shift those memories when they arise. Instead of saying, "This is not enough," try saying, "Wow, I really had this." "I really got to love them." "This hurts deeply, but I'm grateful You allowed me to love them." "Lord, thank You for the time, and thank You for what I have to hold on to."

The shift may not stop the tears, but it *will* shift your spirit toward gratitude—which is sure to drive that spirit of taunt out!

I love you.

Scripture: Isaiah 46:9 (HCSB)
"Remember what happened long ago, for I am God, and there is no other; I am God, and no one is like Me."

God calls us to remember. He knows that our memories are powerful and meaningful. They are not meant to harm us but to remind us of the blessings, the love, and the relationships He allowed us to experience. When we lose someone we love, our memories of them become a gift—a bridge between what was and what still remains in our hearts.

This verse reminds us that just as we are to recall God's faithfulness, we are also to cherish the moments and people He placed in our lives. Rather than viewing memories as painful reminders of loss, we can see them as evidence of love, joy, and the lasting imprint someone has left on us.

Affirmation:

"My memories are a blessing, not a burden. They remind me of the love I've shared and the impact my loved one had on my life. I will cherish these memories and allow them to bring comfort, not pain."

Final Thought:

Memories are not meant to hold you hostage in grief; they are meant to carry you forward with love. Every memory you have is proof that the person you love mattered, that their presence shaped you, and that their love still lingers in your heart. Hold onto these memories, not as a source of sorrow, but as a way to celebrate the love that will never fade.

DON'T BE AFRAID OF YOUR EMOTIONS.

The emotions that grief brings can feel overwhelming—too big to handle or too much to bear. But don't be afraid of what you're experiencing. During the grieving process, you'll encounter familiar emotions in ways you've never felt before. Grief has a way of making you recall the love you shared with someone while simultaneously stirring up anger, simply because they're no longer here. Allow yourself to feel what you're feeling.

There may be moments when peace is accompanied by tears. You might experience a wave of depression just after feeling happy. The world that once seemed so light may suddenly feel engulfed in darkness. This is normal. There's no neat or predictable way to compartmentalize your emotions when it comes to grief.

Think of it as a big, unorganized puzzle with all the pieces scattered on the floor. You're tasked with picking them up and trying to fit them back together. Now imagine those pieces are worn, rugged, and damaged, making it nearly impossible to complete the puzzle perfectly. Even if you manage to piece it together, it might not look the way it once did, and some parts may still not fit quite right. That's what grief looks like—the daily attempt to make sense of it all, only to realize that it still doesn't look or feel the way you thought it would.

Your emotions may not feel "normal" for a long time, and that's okay. Allow yourself the space to process them. Create room for new emotions that you may have never felt before.

Understand that these feelings are not here to defeat you. They exist because you've experienced something meaningful, something worth feeling deeply about.

Grief brings all these emotions forward, not to break you, but to help you redefine what feeling looks like as you move forward. Don't fear your emotions. Address them, welcome them, and correct them when necessary. Give them space—but not more space than they deserve.

Don't aim to be "normal." Instead, aim to be someone who is trying—one step, one feeling at a time.

Your emotions are not in control. You are.

Will there be days when you give in to what you're feeling? Absolutely. But it's a decision you get to make.

Remember this: as crippling as your emotions may feel, you are not crippled. You are not lame. You are not broken. And you are certainly not alone.

Your emotions are fueled by how much power you allow them to have. Please don't strive to not feel them—deal with them. For some, that "dealing" may require professional help. For others, it's learning what daily adjusting looks like. Either way, don't be afraid. God is with you. He is here to help you manage these emotions.

Prayer still works in the midst of grief. It's not just a powerful tool—it's a weapon. Your emotions are defeatable. You are more than a conqueror through Christ Jesus.

Fight your emotions with the Word of God. Cover yourself in His truth—it helps.

Don't fear what you're feeling. This is not your end.

I love You.

Scripture: Psalm 34:18 (NLT)
"The Lord is close to the brokenhearted; he rescues those whose spirits are crushed."

Grief can make emotions feel unbearable—like a storm that never ends. But this verse reminds us that even in our most painful moments, God is near. He does not leave us alone in our brokenness. Instead, He stays close, offering comfort and rescuing us when the weight of sorrow feels too heavy to bear.

This scripture encourages us to stop suppressing our emotions and allow ourselves to feel everything grief brings. Because in the midst of our deepest sadness, God is already at work—soothing, healing, and carrying us through.

Affirmation

"I am not alone in my grief. My emotions are not my enemy. I give myself permission to feel, knowing that God is close to me and guiding me through this journey."

Final Thought:

Grief is messy. It does not follow a perfect pattern, nor does it fit into a timeline. Your emotions are real, valid, and necessary. Don't rush to make sense of them. Instead, trust that even as you feel broken, God is piecing you back together in ways you cannot yet see.

ENJOY THE HAPPY TIMES AS THEY COME AND EMBRACE THE SAD ONES TOO. THEY'RE PROOF YOUR HEART IS WORKING.

Don't feel guilty for wanting to do everyday, normal things to make yourself feel okay or better. And don't be afraid if you also don't feel like participating in certain activities. Grief is complex, and the people who love you—the ones still here—will often try their hardest to help you feel better. They'll do things to make you smile, and that's okay. It's also okay if those attempts don't work.

The people who truly care about you will understand if you say no, and they'll respect your boundaries. They'll also understand if you change your mind. When moments of happiness come, allow yourself to enjoy them. Do things that take you out of your usual routine, even if you feel out of place.

No matter how displaced or broken you may feel, take a moment to embrace something that brings you joy. This is advice I offer from personal experience—I know how this feels. But I also know that enjoying happy moments can sometimes trigger other emotions. It's possible to feel survivor's remorse or be reminded of the things you can no longer do with the person you've lost.

Still, don't stop enjoying the things you both used to love. Let the moments that naturally make you smile happen. And when the tears come, let them flow.

Grief has a way of sneaking up on you—one moment, your day is going well, and the next, you find yourself crying because you realize your heart is broken and you're still deeply sad. This is okay.

Embrace the happy times as best you can and know that the sad moments are just as normal. It's okay to not be happy all the time. It's okay for life to not feel normal. It's okay to miss someone so deeply that it leaves you wanting to shut everything else out for the rest of the day. These feelings are are natural, and they're welcome.

What's important is to try to remain as in control of these emotions as you can. To embrace something means to accept that it has the potential to affect you deeply.

Enjoy the happy times, no matter how fleeting they may be. And embrace the moments that make the tears fall, that make you scream, that make you angry, or that leave you feeling numb. All of it is part of the process, and all of it is okay.

Create happy times. You know what you need better than anyone else. Even if you can't clearly think of what that is right now—TRY. The experimenting process alone can keep your mind moving and your heart open. I'm encouraging you to try.

Create happy moments. Plan happy moments. No matter how small, do things you think you might love. Do things you know you need. If you don't feel like leaving the house or getting out of bed, that's okay. Just open the blinds or crack a window—let in some sunlight and fresh air. As natural as it is to sulk, try not to add to the weight of what you're already feeling.

If you need a day to rest, take it. But don't sit in the dark all day. Play music. Try a new recipe. Step outside for some air. Sit on the porch. Go for a walk. Watch a feel-good movie.
The goal isn't to erase your grief. It's to give your heart a healthy place to rest amidst it.

I don't care how temporary the moment is—create it. Laugh on purpose. There's still something funny. The sun is still shining.
You're still breathing. Just try. It will make a difference—I promise.

I love you.

Scripture: Romans 12:15 (HCSB)
"Rejoice with those who rejoice; weep with those who weep."

Grief doesn't follow a straight path. Some days, you may feel like yourself again, and other days, the weight of loss might leave you feeling drained. This scripture reminds us that emotions are meant to be experienced. It is okay to celebrate life's joyful moments, just as it is okay to cry when grief hits.

You don't have to feel guilty for laughing, smiling, or feeling joy after a loss. And you don't have to feel ashamed when sadness returns. The people who truly love you will understand both sides of grief—the joy and the sorrow—and they will walk with you through it all.

Affirmation:
"I give myself permission to embrace both joy and sorrow. I will not feel guilty for feeling happy, nor will I suppress my sadness. Both are part of healing, and I am allowed to experience them fully."

Final Thought:
You are allowed to feel everything—both the laughter and the tears, the good days and the unbearable ones. There is no right or wrong way to grieve. Let happiness in when it comes, and let sadness flow when it needs to. Healing does not mean forgetting—it means learning how to live with both love and loss in the same heart.

FEEL THE REAL FEELINGS THAT YOU ARE HAVING.

Your feelings are real, and they matter! The way you feel directly impacts how you communicate and interact with others each day. Don't let anyone dismiss or downplay your emotions—but also, be sure you're not dismissing them yourself.

Feelings are meant to affect you. Grief has a way of bringing out raw emotions—ones you may not have even known were within you. It pushes you into a space of unfamiliarity, introducing feelings that might be completely foreign. You may not be used to crying, and suddenly, you can't stop. Perhaps you've never experienced depression, and now you feel unable to get off the couch.

Allow yourself to feel these emotions as they arise. The only way to address them is to acknowledge their presence. By doing so, you create the freedom to understand and navigate them. For instance, if you recognize feelings of depression, you might decide it's time to reach out to someone for help. If you feel the weight of mourning, you might notice you need extra rest. These feelings are guides, helping you process what you're experiencing.

The ability to feel deeply is a sign of how profoundly you've been affected—because you loved.

These emotions don't need to be bottled up to make others more comfortable, nor should you suppress them just because they make you uncomfortable. Your feelings exist to teach you how to navigate the space you're in.

While your emotions can influence your attitude, strive not to let them overshadow your gratitude. Loving someone and feeling grief is not a punishment. These feelings aren't here to make you sulk or to punish you—they're here to remind you of the depth of love you've experienced.

Feelings keep us connected: to God, to ourselves, and to the love we've shared. They show us the magnitude of what it means to care for someone deeply.

Don't fear your feelings. Embrace them, address them, and release the ones you no longer wish to carry. And don't hesitate to seek help for the emotions that feel beyond your control.

The key to all of this is that you have to be honest with yourself about what you're actually feeling. To acknowledge, you must accept that this is happening. The point isn't to push you into a place of pain—it's to help you handle the space you're in by allowing you to face your feelings head-on. This kind of honesty will give you tools for coping when the emotions return—because they will.

Being honest with yourself can feel heavy, especially if you're used to being in control of your emotions. But grief is invasive. It doesn't ask permission before showing up, and it often brings other emotions along with it. Don't be embarrassed if you don't have all the answers. Ask for help. If you feel overwhelmed, please don't suffer at the hands of your feelings alone.

Feeling your emotions isn't the same as suffering—it's about acknowledging what's real. Please don't believe the lie that you're in this alone or that you've been left in darkness. You are loved more than you know. Don't feel alone—pun intended. You are surrounded by more than just your emotions. The love and support around you are bigger than what you're feeling.

I love you.

Scripture: Psalm 34:18 (NLT)
"The Lord is close to the brokenhearted; he rescues those whose spirits are crushed."

God does not dismiss your emotions, and neither should you. When you are hurting, when grief is overwhelming, when emotions feel too heavy to bear—God is near. He sees your pain, acknowledges your feelings, and remains close to you.

Your emotions are valid. They are not a sign of weakness, nor are they something to ignore. Instead, they serve as reminders of love, connection, and the impact someone had on your life. Rather than suppressing what you feel, take comfort in knowing that even in your hardest moments, God is holding you through them.

Affirmation:

"I honor my emotions and allow myself to feel them fully. My grief is not a burden, and my emotions do not define me. God is near, and He walks with me through every feeling I experience."

Final Thought:

Grief will introduce emotions that feel unfamiliar, and some days, they may seem unbearable. But just as deep as your pain goes, so does God's love and comfort. Your emotions matter. They are reminders of your love, your humanity, and your connection to something greater than yourself. Feel what you need to feel—but do not carry it alone.

GRIEF WILL LOOK DIFFERENT EVERY SINGLE DAY.

Waking up to sunny skies only to step outside and find it gloomy and rainy—that's what grief can feel like every single day. Living daily life while grieving means understanding that each minute, hour, and day can bring a completely different emotional landscape. One moment you may be laughing, and the next, you're crying. Anger can shift to sadness, and feeling motivation to be productive can turn into a desire to isolate yourself.

Grief looks different for everyone and every day. There will be days when you feel energized and ready to take on the world, and other days when you want to close yourself off entirely. Some days, you might feel capable of supporting others, while on other days, you may not have a single encouraging word to share.

It's essential not to compare your grief to someone else's. The way you feel is unique to you, and it's valid. Grief manifesting differently every day doesn't mean it's in control of you. Instead, it signifies that you have a safe space to feel whatever you need to feel in the moment.

This process will look different for everyone—adults and children alike. For some, it might manifest as a desire to lash out (though it's not recommended). For others, it might provoke hard but necessary conversations.

Grief can feel isolating, as though no one truly understands your pain or the depth of your heartbreak. It may even feel like a constant battle to articulate what you're going through or to figure out what the next moment should look like. While grief can deeply affect your mood, it's not meant to control you. Do your best not to end the day the same way it started—unless it began on a positive note.

Strive to start your day with as much positivity as possible, and aim to end it by finding something, however small, to be thankful for.

Conditioning your mind to resist adapting to every mood grief may bring is crucial for your well-being. At times, it may feel like you're losing control, but learning to manage how grief affects your mood can ultimately shape what the next moment, hour, or day looks like.

While you are not in control of the next moment, you are in control of how you respond to it. Grief is going to look different moment by moment. This is because of the vulnerability attached to it. If you're not used to being vulnerable, this adapting may seem even more difficult.

The trying times of the day can feel like they're affecting you more than usual. The overstimulation can feel like no other. But the way you choose to respond to this will affect what the next moments—*the ones you can control*—will look like.

The day is not here to break you. Don't run from it. Don't be so eager to confront it, either. Give these feelings the response they deserve. Only you know what that looks like. It may mean taking the day. It may mean an impulse need for comfort, or even a necessary need for temporary disconnection.

It is very important to not just disengage. Make sure you're communicating this to someone. This desire is not wrong. Just don't let it become too often. You know what you need.

Grief has need of you to thrive. Starve it in the ways you can —by not adhering to its rules as best you can.
Allow grief to look different every day, but don't allow it to *change you daily*. There's a you that we still need in our lives, and a *you* that you still deserve to be. Adapt. Don't change.

I love you.

Scripture: Lamentations 3:22-23 (ESV)
"The steadfast love of the Lord never ceases; his mercies never come to an end; they are new every morning; great is your faithfulness."

Every day brings new emotions, and with grief, those emotions can feel like an unpredictable storm. Some mornings, you might wake up feeling strong, while others, you might struggle to get out of bed. But this verse reminds us that no matter what yesterday felt like, God's mercies are new every single morning. His love for you hasn't changed just because you're grieving. His grace is there, waiting for you to receive it.

Grief will try to convince you that you are stuck in a never-ending cycle of pain, but you don't have to let it define you. You are allowed to feel everything that comes with it, but you are also allowed to seek peace, to find moments of joy, and to remind yourself that each day is a fresh start.

Affirmation:
"I will allow myself to feel, but I will not let grief control me. I wake up each day with new mercy, new grace, and new strength. No matter how I feel, I am not alone."

Final Thought:
Grief may shift your emotions unexpectedly, but you don't have to be at its mercy. God's love is unchanging, even when your feelings aren't. No matter how your day starts, remember that you have the power to choose how it ends.

HEALING LOOKS AND SOUNDS DIFFERENT FOR EVERYBODY.

Healing hurts. Healing is messy. Healing is not fun. Healing is a journey—a process.

When it comes to grief, the purpose of healing isn't to forget. Instead, it's about learning to adjust to a new normal that you never anticipated. Healing takes time, and it looks different for everyone.

Healing might mean journaling your thoughts and emotions. It might mean stepping outside to get fresh air or making sure you're eating properly. Sometimes, healing requires answering those difficult phone calls you've been avoiding or spending quiet time alone. Other times, it's about doing things that bring you joy.

The healing journey through grief also means accepting that there may always be a void. Losing someone creates a space in your heart that can feel impossible to fill. It's not easy to face the daily reality that they're not coming back—that you can't see them, call them, or send them a message. You can't share a funny video, seek their advice, or hear their voice.

Healing means tending to that hole in your heart. While it may never fully close, you can learn to fill it with things that bring beauty, joy, and meaning. That's what healing looks like. It's important to remember that healing is deeply personal.

What you need to heal might be completely different from what someone else needs—even if you've both lost the same person. While you might need to be cared for, someone else might need space. You may find comfort in laughter and uplifting moments, while another person might need solitude to cry and process their emotions.

Healing is unique because each person who touches our lives affects us differently. When they're no longer here, our paths to healing reflect the unique ways they impacted us.

As challenging and messy as the healing process may be, it has the potential to create something beautiful—a life rebuilt with love, memories, and hope.

This is not a healing to forget or a healing to "get over it." This healing is the opening of letting God come in and heal through mending--healing what hurts through love. This healing doesn't lead to the forgetting; it leads to the sustainable wholesomeness of our hearts. It is us bringing the aching of grief in our hearts and spirit to God, not for him to "fix" but for Him to console, comfort and rescue.

This healing doesn't restore what's been lost, but it does piece our hearts back together with peace.

What are you filling this hole with? If you aren't careful, it will begin to fill itself with things that aren't helpful to healthy healing. Leaving a void in control to fill itself will only cause it to fill with the things that already feel like they're defeating you—because the noise of it is already loud.

Take control of this filling process. You are the garden and the gardener. Plant beautiful things.
Beauty still exists in the ugliness of grief. The wrong seeds can ruin you and your progress. Be careful of what you're allowing people to plant into you—it matters. Protect this open space as best as you can. God has beautiful things to fill and restore you with. Let Him.

Fill yourself with things that bring you joy, peace, love, hope, faith, and structure. It's important to be strategic about what you're filling yourself with. The blooming may not make the void worth it, but it will show you that you are capable of maneuvering through transition—beautifully, even in the midst of things that don't feel so beautiful.

I love you.

Scripture: Psalm 147:3 (HCSB)
"He heals the brokenhearted and binds up their wounds."

Healing from grief is not easy, and it's often painful. It doesn't happen overnight, and it doesn't look the same for everyone. But this scripture reminds us of an important truth—God is in the business of healing. He doesn't rush our healing or demand that we move on before we're ready. Instead, He gently tends to our wounds, binding them up so they don't remain open forever.

Grief may leave you feeling shattered, but God is patient with your pain. He walks with you through the messiness, through the tears, through the moments when healing feels impossible. Even when the void in your heart remains, He helps you fill it with love, purpose, and hope.

Affirmation:
"I am healing, even when it feels slow. I will not compare my healing journey to others. My pain is real, but so is my ability to grow through it. God is with me in every step."

Final Thought:
Healing doesn't mean forgetting. It means adjusting, creating space for joy in the midst of sorrow, and allowing God to work through the pain. Be patient with yourself. Healing is not about perfection—it's about progress.

IT REALLY WILL BE OK.

As cliché as it may sound, it's true: It will be okay. But let's be honest—that's not something easy to hold onto or even believe. When your life feels like it's falling apart, those words might seem hollow, distant, or even frustrating. In the moment, and in the days to come, it may not feel like anything will ever be "okay" again. But I'm here to tell you this: sometimes, just being okay is enough. It's not about life returning to "normal," because it likely never will. It may never feel as blissful as you remember. It may never be as perfect as it once seemed. But even so, it can be okay—in the truest, most literal sense of the word.

When you take time to sit with the idea, you might come to understand that okay is not only acceptable—it's meaningful. When I say, It will be okay, I'm not suggesting perfection or the resolution of all pain. I'm saying that things can shift to a place where they're manageable, even if they're never the same.

"Okay" might not feel extraordinary, but it's a state of learning, adapting, and adjusting. It's about finding a way to exist within a new reality that feels foreign and unfair. You may not ever feel blissful in this area of loss again, but you can still feel okay. And okay is enough.

Okay is simply a declaration: I am learning to adjust. It's a response to life's uncertainties, an acknowledgment that you're finding your footing in the midst of instability. It's okay to not be okay. When someone asks, How are you? and all you can muster is, I'm just okay, that's valid. You don't need to pressure yourself into saying more. There's no urgency to rush past this stage or pretend to feel something you don't.

"Okay" doesn't mean life has lost its beauty. It doesn't mean you're stagnant or failing to move forward. Okay doesn't negate progress or joy. Instead, it means you're allowing yourself the grace to function, to breathe, and to exist in a space that once seemed impossible.

Over time, your language might evolve. Someday, you may say, I'm good, or I'm at peace. But until then, "okay" is enough. It's a place of healing, a steppingstone that allows you to process the pain without the pressure to move too quickly.

So yes, life might look and feel different forever. Things may never return to the way they were, and that's a painful truth to accept. But okay means you're learning to adjust, to navigate a reality you didn't choose but are determined to live within. It really will be okay. And that's okay.

"Okay" doesn't have to be a forever feeling. Coming to terms with the fact that your loved one is not coming back can make you feel like life will forever remain dull or that you'll never be the same, but "okay" can turn back into "I'm starting to feel like myself again." Nothing about the loss has changed, but I am feeling good now. I'm okay with the fact that I'm here and living day by day.

The steps to this feeling have no step-by-step path. You can wake up one day and feel amazing. This is all about learning to manage grief, not mask it. "I'm doing okay. I'm not okay with what I am experiencing, but I am okay in the aspect that I am embracing good days." "With a missing component, things are feeling more normal, more natural. I'm showing up." "I'm okay, and God's got me." Don't be afraid to proclaim the emotions tied to how you're feeling on good days. "I feel good" is okay!

People are not expecting you to feel down forever. Seeing you smile will make them smile. People are praying for your joy daily—I know I am. So when it comes, as often as it comes, don't just welcome it—shout it aloud! I love you.

Scripture: 2 Corinthians 12:9 (NLT)

"Each time he said, 'My grace is all you need. My power works best in weakness.' So now I am glad to boast about my weaknesses, so that the power of Christ can work through me."

This verse reminds us that we don't have to be strong on our own. We don't have to have it all figured out. When life feels unbearable, when grief is overwhelming, and when we feel like "okay" is the best we can manage—that is enough. God's grace fills the gaps where we feel broken.

Being "okay" doesn't mean the pain is gone, but it does mean that God's strength is carrying us through. It means we are still standing, still breathing, and still pushing forward, even if it's hard.

Affirmation:
"I don't have to have it all together. God's grace is enough for me. I am learning to be okay, and that is enough for today."

Final Thought:
Healing doesn't happen overnight, and perfection isn't the goal. Some days, simply making it through is an accomplishment. "Okay" is a place of progress, not defeat.

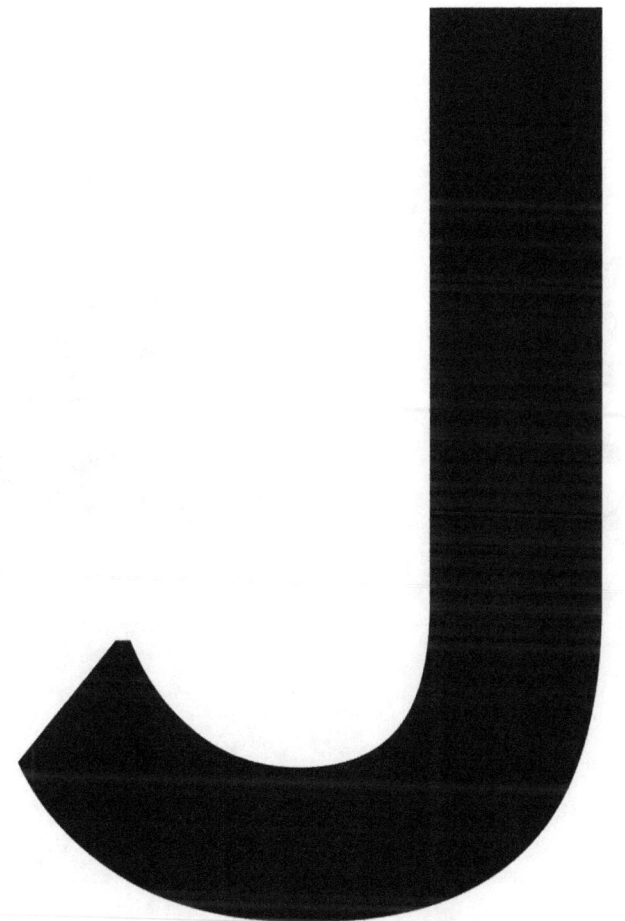

JESUS IS SO CLOSE TO YOU.

You have not been forsaken. The Bible reminds us that God promises never to leave us or forsake us, and even in grief, that promise remains true. Losing a loved one and experiencing the emotions that come with it can make us feel like God has forgotten us. But I want to remind you: He is still near to the brokenhearted. His promise to be close isn't based on circumstances or time—it's His unchanging character. Even as you navigate the pain of grief, Jesus is near. He knows every detail about you, from the hairs on your head to the plans He has for your life. He is more than able to bring you comfort.

Sometimes, losing someone can feel like punishment. It's easy to think God has taken them from us as a way to chastise us. But that is not who God is. God does not punish us through death. The loss of your loved one is not God trying to harm you. In fact, He loves you so deeply that He helps you move through grief, even when it feels impossible.

It's natural to feel angry or blame God for the loss, but we often do this without understanding that every person has their own journey. Some people finish their race earlier than others, whether due to tragic, unexpected circumstances or after a long, full life. No matter how or when we lose someone, the pain is real, and the blow is never softened. Even with a broken heart, God desires to be near and to heal you.

Let Him be your heart-mender and your peacekeeper. That's who He is—unchanging and constant. Not even grief can change His love for you. The Bible says that nothing can separate us from the love of Christ—not death, not life, not anything else.

God's promise is true: He will never leave you or forsake you. He will be with you, even until the end of time. Take a moment today to let Him be near, and see how His love can change your heart and bring you peace.

Don't believe the lies of the devil. He is still, in fact, the enemy—here to taunt your mind with false evidence that appears real. His job is to deceive you with the lie that Jesus doesn't like you and that He's punishing you. These lies are to keep you from the resting arms of Christ. Don't fall for the deception. If you can be convinced that Jesus is not near you, you'll be convinced that you are in this alone.
You are still in good company—in Christ. He loves you so much.

Remember this: Jesus knows what death feels like. Besides experiencing it in real time Himself, the Bible gives account of the instance where the idea of death even weighed Him down as He journeyed to Calvary. In another account, we see where He cried tears associated with death.

Don't you dare believe that Jesus would leave you to fend for yourself with the grappling agony death brings. He knows exactly what it is and what it feels like. So much so, that in His own death, He left a Comforter—the Holy Spirit—to dwell with us.

Jesus is not "not close" to you, and you are not alone. God is mindful. And the devil is a liar—a manipulating antagonist who has no rights in your story of grief.

I don't care how easy it is to disconnect because of your emotions—cling to Jesus, because He is clinging to you!

I love you!

Scripture: Psalm 34:18 (HCSB)

"The Lord is near the brokenhearted; He saves those crushed in spirit."

Grief has a way of making us feel completely alone, as if God has turned His back on us. But Psalm 34:18 reminds us that even in our darkest moments, God is not far—He is closer than ever. He doesn't just watch from a distance; He actively saves and comforts those who are crushed by loss.

This means that no matter how deep the pain feels, God has not abandoned you. His presence is constant, and His love is unshakable. You don't have to carry your grief alone—God is holding you, even when you feel too weak to stand.

Affirmation:
"I am not alone in my grief. God is near, comforting me and holding me through my pain. His love is my refuge, and His presence brings me peace."

Final Thought:
Grief does not mean you are forsaken. God's love is not conditional, and He is not punishing you through loss. Allow yourself to rest in His promise that He is near. Even in brokenness, He is working to mend your heart.

KEEPING YOUR FEELINGS INSIDE IS NOT HEALTHY. FIND A HEALTHY OUTLET.

Sometimes we keep our feelings bottled up because we worry about how they might affect others. While it's important not to lash out, holding everything inside can hurt you in the long run.

Grief can make you feel like shutting down. It might make you want to be alone, avoid others, or even speak unkindly to people without meaning to. Grief is a consumer! If you let it, grief can consume you—it can even make you feel sick. That's why it's so important to find healthy ways to cope.

Think about something you enjoy or used to enjoy. Maybe there's an activity you loved as a child that you could try again, or maybe there's something new you've always wanted to do. Find something to help you as you adjust. People might say to "get your mind off of it," but let's be real—your mind will always be on what you're experiencing. Instead, focus on giving your mind something healthy to do.

Go see a movie. Read a book. Try karaoke. Go to a concert. Do something fun and even a little silly that makes you smile. The point isn't to forget your grief—it's to give yourself a healthy outlet for your emotions.

When looking for support, be careful not to rely too much on one person for comfort. Instead of forming unhealthy bonds of codependency, invite someone to join you in an activity—something that helps you feel better and keeps you moving forward.

Healthy outlets help balance the heavy emotions inside. They won't change what you're going through, but they can make it easier to handle.

Sometimes you won't be able to express your feelings exactly how you'd like, but finding a healthy alternative—a way to release those feelings—can improve your mental and emotional state.

Don't keep your emotions bottled up. If you hold them inside, they can take over. Instead, find ways to let them out in a way that helps you heal.

You are not a burden to the people who want to see you happy. Invite people to do things with you. Accept healthy invitations.

If your emotions don't have a healthy outlet, it will only be a matter of time before you combust! You must let out the steam of your emotions. This is tricky because no one can make you do it. You have to learn when you need to blow off the steam. Only you know when it's too much—don't push yourself to that edge before you let it out.

Decompression is key. Decompress daily—sometimes multiple times a day. Do more than scroll... take a stroll. Start a TV show or movie series. Start a DIY project. Do something that's attached to progress so the neglect of it becomes obvious. This helps keep you accountable. Start a book. Do something you can intentionally invest yourself in.

This is also where things like book clubs and networking events come into play—maybe even trying a support group. Find something that helps you track your time and keeps you consistent. You have to have a healthy outlet. You don't always need someone to do these things with you, but partnership and community do help—and they also make sure you don't spend too much time alone.

Journal as often as you can—whether it's writing out your prayers or your emotions. I personally love digital journaling. Video record yourself in the morning with how you feel, and then again in the evening with a lesson you learned, how God spoke to you that day, or just how you feel compared to how you started. It helps you stay on top of taking care of you.

Do what's best for you.
I love you.

Scripture: Matthew 11:28 (ESV)
"Come to me, all who labor and are heavy laden, and I will give you rest."

Grief is heavy, and carrying the weight of your emotions alone can feel overwhelming. Matthew 11:28 is Jesus' reminder that you don't have to hold everything inside—He invites you to bring your burdens to Him. He offers rest, not just physical rest, but emotional and spiritual peace.

This means that instead of bottling up your feelings, you can lay them down before God. You don't have to pretend to be okay or carry the weight of grief alone. He sees what you're going through, and He wants to give you relief in ways that the world cannot.

Affirmation:
"I do not have to carry my grief alone. God offers me rest, comfort, and peace. I will find healthy ways to express my emotions and allow myself to heal."

Final Thought:
Your emotions deserve space to be felt, processed, and released. Don't let grief consume you—find ways to express what's inside, whether through prayer, activities, or trusted connections. God has given you healthy outlets to help you heal, and He is always there to carry the weight when it feels too heavy.

LOVE HAS NOT BEEN TAKEN AWAY FROM YOU. IT JUST LOOKS A LITTLE DIFFERENT NOW.

You are so loved, and you matter more than you know. Your heart is so important. You are the reason so many people find the strength to get up every day. You are the reason so many people smile. You are the reason some people have the faith they do.

Don't ever think that this loss means you are unloved—it doesn't. You are deeply loved, and you have loved so deeply in return. I know it feels different right now, but your ability to love still exists. Even if you're unsure what love looks like right now, remember this: you still have so much love to give.

Love hasn't been taken away from you. It's still there; it just looks different now. Loving someone is one of the greatest gifts we get, and it's hard because we don't get to choose when the physical expression of that love comes to an end.

But love doesn't stop. Love is forever. Even when someone is no longer close to us, we can find new ways to love them and carry them in our hearts. That love doesn't go away—it grows and transforms, becoming a part of who we are.

God is still sending people to love you—and people for you to love back. Please don't let the fear that grief brings cause you to push them away.

Grief has a way of making you obsess over the time you have "left" with people. It can make you "over-love" them out of fear that they're leaving next. This is not healthy, and this is not love. I pray that God removes that feeling from you—the one that causes you to love from a place of panic.

That kind of fear steals the authenticity from the time you spend with others, making it hard to enjoy the moment. Don't love people like they're going to leave you (I don't care how true that may feel). Love them like you have them today, and do it day by day.

Keep your love pure. Spend more time where it matters, and be intentional about telling people that you love them. Make the time count—but try not to obsess over counting it.

I love you.

Scripture: Romans 8:38-39 (NLT)

"And I am convinced that nothing can ever separate us from God's love. Neither death nor life, neither angels nor demons, neither our fears for today nor our worries about tomorrow—not even the powers of hell can separate us from God's love. No power in the sky above or in the earth below—indeed, nothing in all creation will ever be able to separate us from the love of God that is revealed in Christ Jesus our Lord."

Grief can make you feel like love has been taken away, but God reminds us that love never ends. Not even death can separate us from love—love from God, or the love we shared with our person. The love you gave and received didn't vanish the moment they left this world. It still exists in your heart, in your memories, and in the impact they had on your life.

This verse is a reminder that love is stronger than anything—including death. Love remains. Love is forever. Just as God's love never leaves us, neither does the love of those we have lost.

Affirmation:
"I am loved. Love has not been taken from me—it has only changed form. I carry love in my heart always, and nothing can separate me from it."

Final Thought:
Losing someone you love doesn't mean losing love itself. The love you shared still exists—it's woven into the fabric of who you are. Hold onto that love, knowing that it is as real now as it ever was. Love does not end.

MEMORIES STAY ALIVE FOREVER!

Tell funny stories about your loved one to as many people as you can. Share memories of special holidays, birthdays, and awkward or funny moments you experienced together. Talk about a time they made you laugh until you cried or a moment when they made you feel safe and loved. These memories are treasures, and as long as you keep telling them, they stay alive.

Sharing memories with younger children helps them get to know someone who has passed on. Tell them the little details: the way this person laughed, their favorite style of clothes, how they danced, or how their voice sounded. These stories help bring the person to life in their minds, even if they never got to meet them.

Don't stop telling these stories. This is how you keep their memory alive. The moments you shared, the love you felt, and the joy they brought into your life can be remembered for years and years. Memories don't die—they are part of your spirit and your story.

Take time to reflect on these memories, even if you're alone. Think about the times they made you feel loved or encouraged you. Remember the experiences you had together, the things you did for the first time with them, and even the tough moments that taught you something important.

These memories are a gift. They can inspire you to create new moments with the people you love who are still here. Just because someone is no longer physically with you doesn't mean they're gone from your life. It's your job to keep their memory alive in your heart.

For some, it's hard to talk about loved ones in the past tense. It might feel more natural to speak of them as if they're still here, as if you're expecting a phone call or planning another trip together. That's okay. Memories remind us that time doesn't erase the love we've shared.

Celebrate their birthdays and milestones, even if they're not physically present. Hold onto these things, even the ones that make you sad, not to dwell on the pain, but to honor the love and connection you shared. Remember how much they loved you, how special they were to you, and how they continue to be a part of you.

Don't let their memory fade because you stop talking about them. Speak their name, share their stories, and keep them alive in your heart. Memories aren't meant to torture you—they're meant to remind you of the love and joy you shared.

The best part is that you get to see the memories exactly the way you need to—whether in daydreams or conversations with others. Again, while memories are not enough, they are yours for the keeping. Your memories don't experience death. They belong to you, and no one can take them from you.

It is important to always remember! The more you recall, the fresher those memories will remain. Stay sharp in your mind about who this person was. Remember the small details—the laughs, recipes, favorites, inside jokes. All of it matters! God gives us memories to remember. Hold on to them. They bring realness to the fact that the person you miss existed.

Scripture: Proverbs 10:7 (NLT)
"We have happy memories of the godly, but the name of a wicked person rots away."

Memories are a gift. They remind us of the love, joy, and impact our loved ones had on our lives. This verse teaches us that those who lived with kindness and love leave behind a legacy that remains in our hearts. Talking about them, sharing their stories, and keeping their memory alive is a way of honoring them.

Your loved one made a difference in your life, and those memories are worth keeping alive. Speaking their name, telling their stories, and reflecting on their love does not mean you are stuck in grief—it means their impact continues.

Affirmation:

"The memories I have of my loved one are a gift. I will share their stories, speak their name, and keep their love alive in my heart."

Final Thought:

Keeping someone's memory alive is not about living in the past—it's about carrying their love forward. Share their laughter, wisdom, and kindness. Every time you tell a story, they live on.

NEVER STOP PRAYING. NO MATTER HOW HARD IT MAY GET, NEVER STOP PRAYING. INCLUDE YOURSELF IN THOSE PRAYERS AS WELL.

Don't let grief take away your prayer life. Grieving is hard, but there's nothing in this world we can truly do without prayer and trust in God. Even when it feels like you don't have the words to say, don't stop communicating with Him. The Bible reminds us that in our hardest times, even our moans and groans are understood by God. Jesus Himself intercedes for us, making sure our hearts are heard.

Don't let grief make you feel too far from God. He is still here. He is still listening, still understanding, and still ready to heal your heart. Prayer is what connects us to Him—it keeps us close. It's how we talk to Him and how He speaks back to us. In prayer, God can give us what we need, even when we're hurting. He can bring healing, clarity, and even peace.

Prayer isn't just about asking for things or expressing our pain. It's also a way to remind ourselves that God is still good. Even in grief, God deserves to hear our voice, to hear us call on Him, and to hear us speak well of Him.

If you're struggling to find the words to pray, start small. Say, "Thank you." Say, "God, help me." Say, "I need you." Say, "I'm grateful for the time I had with the person I love." Your prayers don't have to be long or perfect. Even if all you can do is pray scripture, do that. Pray to protect your mind, your spirit, and your family. Most importantly, don't forget to pray for yourself—for strength, for wisdom, and for guidance in what to do next.

Prayer strengthens us, even when our hearts are heavy. It helps us speak hope into situations that feel hopeless. It helps us see that grief, though it's something we must go through, doesn't have to keep us stuck forever. Prayer is the tool that helps us move forward.

The Bible reminds us that we don't grieve like the world does. We grieve with hope—hope that there is a greater plan, hope that God has brought our loved one to a better place, and hope that they are now at rest in Him in a way this world could never offer.

Take time to pray, even when it's hard. Thank God, ask Him for help, and tell Him how you feel. Be honest with Him—He can handle your frustrations and your pain. God listens to your heart and understands your spirit.

Don't stop praying. Cover yourself, your family, and your future in prayer. Through prayer, God moves on our behalf. Prayer is the connection that keeps us close to Him, even in the darkest times.

No prayer is a dumb one, and no prayer is too small. He wants to hear it all. He wants to meet you in your place of brokenness. Prayer is the only conversation you'll ever have where your tears have words and your groans have definitions. It's a place where your words don't have to make sense, and you don't have to over-express to be understood. Just talk to God.

Remove the "deepness" from it and come bearing your heart—He wants to hear from you. When you speak to Him, you'll start to see how He answers your prayers more clearly. Praying is not about the length; it's about time. The length of your prayer doesn't matter—the time your spirit takes out to talk to God does.

He desires to commune with you. He's not looking to find fault in your requests and communication—He's looking to communicate with you.

Prayer strengthens you. Prayer is fuel. Prayer applies grit to the grieving heart to keep going. Prayer is necessary.

It's coverage for you during this state of vulnerability. Prayer makes you a conqueror and not prey to the enemy.

Be covered.

I am praying for you.

I love you!

Scripture: Romans 8:26 (NLT)

"And the Holy Spirit helps us in our weakness. For example, we don't know what God wants us to pray for. But the Holy Spirit prays for us with groanings that cannot be expressed in words."

Grief can leave us feeling empty, weak, and unable to find the right words to pray. This verse reminds us that God understands our pain, even when we can't articulate it. The Holy Spirit steps in, interceding on our behalf, making sure our hearts are heard.

You don't have to have the perfect words or long prayers—just keep the connection open. Whether it's a sigh, a whisper, or a single word, God hears you.

Affirmation:
"Even when I don't have the words, God hears my heart. My grief will not separate me from Him—prayer will keep me connected to His peace and His presence."

Final Thought:
Grief doesn't have to distance you from God. Even in silence, He is near. Let prayer be your bridge to healing, strength, and peace.

OFFER SUPPORT TO OTHERS WHEN YOU CAN. YOUR LOVE GOES A LONG WAY.

When you're the one everyone depends on, grief can feel even heavier. It might seem like you need to focus on yourself—and that's okay. But supporting others during this time can also help you heal.

I know it can feel unfair, like everyone else gets the space to grieve while you're left holding things together. You might feel like helping others takes away from your chance to fully process your own emotions. But God has equipped you for this role, even during tough times. As you support others, He will also bring people into your life to help you when you need it most.

Grief doesn't wait for anyone—it just happens. Often, you're the one holding everyone else together. That doesn't mean you can't grieve or feel what you need to feel. But your support can make a huge difference in someone else's life. Sometimes, support looks like encouraging words, a hug, a meal, or just being present. Your love and care go farther than you realize.

You are a light. God made you to bring hope and stability to others. Even when it feels hard, this is part of His purpose for you. But know this: God will never let you run empty. As you give to others, He will fill you back up with the strength and peace you need.

It's easy to get frustrated when others rely on you, especially when you're hurting too. Supporting others can sometimes feel like people are unloading their struggles onto you, leaving you unsure of where to put your own feelings. But God won't let you carry these burdens alone. He takes them from you, even if others don't know how to give them to Him. You're simply a vessel—a helper standing in the gap for others.

It's an honor to be a source of strength, even during grief. God hasn't forgotten about you.

He sees you, strengthens you, and ensures you won't be overwhelmed. Offer what you can, where you can, and trust God to guide you. Even small acts of love can have a big impact.

Take time to be kind. Take time to listen. Take time to reflect on how God is using you, even in your pain. He will give you clarity and peace as you serve. Supporting others doesn't take away from your grief—it adds purpose to the journey.

Don't drown yourself so deep in this support that there's no room for others to support you. Make sure you are trying to make room to healthily categorize your emotions and time for rest. This time is still vital to make sure you are being poured into.

Make sure you are making space for your spiritual filling as well. This is so important. Your filling time is something that you are allowed to make a habit—ensure that it is happening for your own good. You can't be of effective support while depleted!

Your support goes a long way, but your filling will keep you standing. It helps you take on what supporting others entails. The only way you can support is if you take time to be fueled! I love you.

Scripture: Galatians 6:2 (NLT)
"Share each other's burdens, and in this way obey the law of Christ."

Grief can feel overwhelming, especially when you're the one everyone turns to for support. This verse reminds us that God calls us to help carry each other's burdens—not by taking on all their weight, but by standing alongside them in love.

If you are the strong one, know that God has given you the ability to uplift others, and He will also send people to uplift you. You are not meant to carry everything alone. Lean on God and allow Him to refill you as you give to others.

Affirmation:
"I am strong, but I am not alone. God sees me, strengthens me, and fills me as I support others. My grief has purpose, and I trust God to guide me through it."

Final Thought:
Your role as a source of strength does not go unnoticed. God sees your heart, your effort, and your pain. He will make sure you are not depleted. Keep showing love, and let Him sustain you.

PEACE IS A FREE GIFT FROM GOD. HE COMFORTS US WITH IT.

When the storms are raging, God is there. When peace feels far away, God is still near.

Remember who your soul is anchored in and the peace that God gives. The Bible tells us that the peace of God guards our hearts and minds. It brings understanding, wisdom, and the strength to move forward. Even in grief, God's peace provides comfort.

God sends His Holy Spirit to be our comforter—someone we can rely on, someone who listens, and someone who holds us when we feel most alone. In the darkest nights, when no one else is there, God's peace is present. In times of struggle, when everything feels overwhelming and there's no help in sight, His peace remains. Even when we can't find the words to express our pain, and all we know is that our hearts are heavy, God's peace is there.

Peace is a part of God's character—it calms our fears and brings stability to our lives. It is a free gift, given to comfort our souls, settle our minds, and bring calm to our spirits. When life feels cloudy, peace brings clarity. When everything feels messy, peace restores order. When we don't know which way to turn, peace gives direction.

God knows our need for peace, even in the midst of chaos. He knows when we need it, where to place it, and how to activate it in our lives. Peace is always available to us—it resides within us because it's something God has given.

Peace helps us sleep at night. It clears our minds of unhealthy thoughts. Just three words—Peace, be still—can calm the storms in our lives. No matter how big the storm of grief may feel, with its rain, winds, and thunder, God commands peace to settle it all.

Peace belongs to you. It is your right. Peace comes from God, and He promises to withhold no good thing from those who walk with Him. Peace is your portion.

I know grieving is hard. I know it's confusing. Sometimes it feels like there are no words for what you're experiencing. But in the midst of confusion, heartbreak, and loss, God sends His peace to guide you every time.

In anger, peace is still there. In sadness, peace is still there. In heartbreak, peace is still there. Peace remains constant through everything we go through because it never leaves us. It's not something you have to beg for—it's a gift from God.

Even in the darkest season, peace is your portion. Peace is a gentle reminder that God is covering you, holding you, and keeping you. No matter what grief brings, God is still in control. He still calms the winds and settles the storms in your life.

The acceptance of peace doesn't have to be understood by way of its concept, but it does have to be intentionally welcomed in! Welcome peace in. Peace may not give back the person we lost, but it does restore what grief has taken.

The only thing peace costs is an exchange for the chaos that's happening. You must be willing to give it up. I know the emotions feel normal now, but peace can help them not consume you!

Make an exchange for peace!

I love you!

Scripture: John 14:27 (AMP)

"Peace I leave with you; My [perfect] peace I give to you; not as the world gives do I give to you. Do not let your heart be troubled, nor let it be afraid [let My perfect peace calm you in every circumstance and give you courage and strength for every challenge]."

Jesus promised His peace to us—a peace that is unlike anything the world can give. This peace is not based on circumstances or fleeting emotions, but on God's unshakable presence. Grief can make you feel like your world is out of control, but even in the hardest moments, God's peace remains steady. It's the kind of peace that calms storms, settles restless hearts, and gives strength to keep moving forward. Even when you don't understand what's happening, trust that God's peace is available to sustain you.

Affirmation:
"God's peace is my anchor. It calms my heart, clears my mind, and gives me strength to move forward. No matter what grief brings, I am covered in His peace."

Final Thought:
Peace is not something you have to chase—it's already yours. Let it fill you, guide you, and bring comfort to your soul. Even in grief, peace is still your portion.

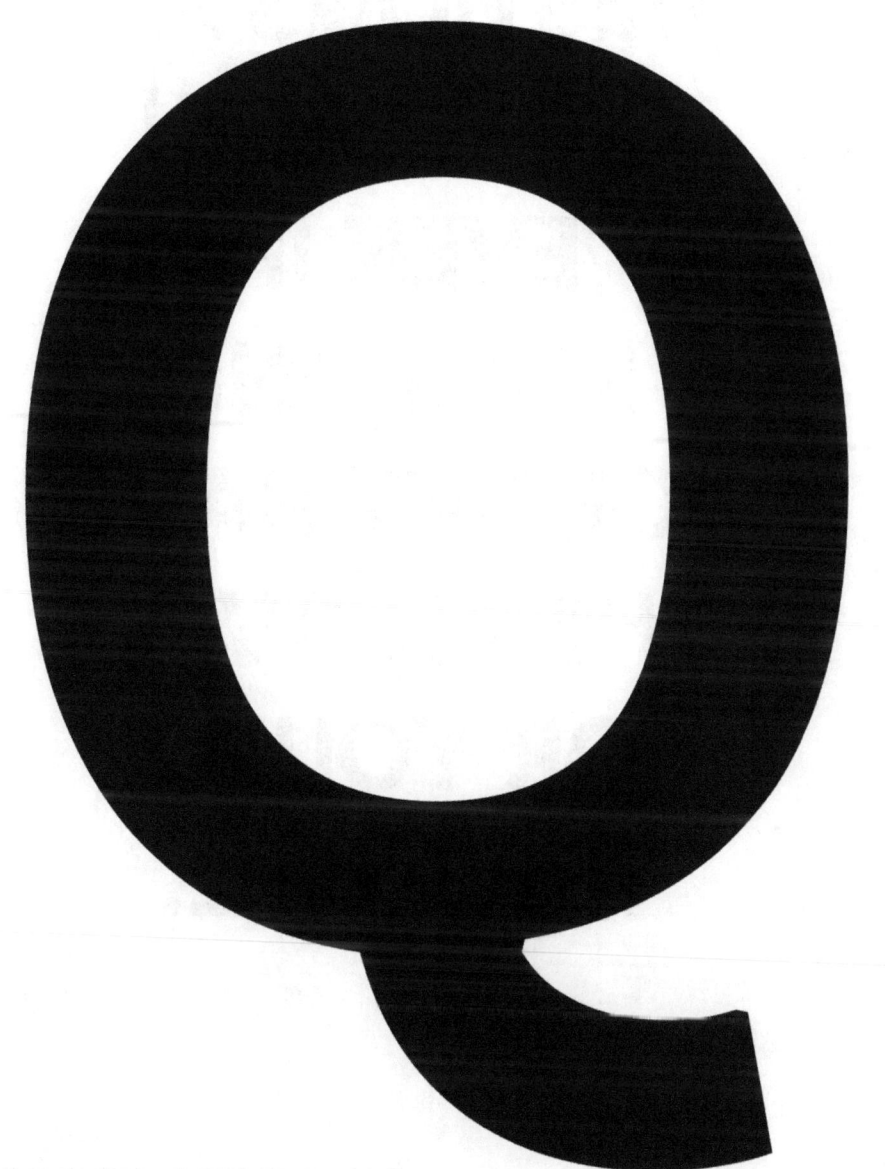

QUESTIONS ARE OK TO ASK! EVEN IF SOMEONE DOESN'T HAVE THE ANSWER FOR YOU AT THAT TIME.

Grief often leaves us with unanswered questions, and that's okay. It's natural to ask "why" when we don't understand, but sometimes those questions don't bring clarity or closure. Sometimes, there are no answers to the questions we ask.

We may never understand why people leave us so soon, why time feels so unfair, or what happens after someone passes. The only thing we can trust is that God doesn't make mistakes. As cliché as that sounds, it's a reminder of His sovereignty. His plans are beyond what we can comprehend. We can't fully grasp His timing or purpose because He is in control.

Submitting to God's plan isn't easy. It's normal to want to ask, "Why?" And it's not wrong to ask God why—He invites us to come to Him with our questions. But we have to be prepared for His answers, even if they don't make sense to us right now. Sometimes, His answer is simply, You'll understand better later.

God doesn't need our permission to act; instead, we need His permission for everything we do. Yet, in His sovereignty, He allows us to approach Him boldly—not disrespectfully, but with confidence. He hears our cries, our confusion, and our need for clarity.

Sometimes, God answers our "why" with love. Sometimes, His answer is peace. Sometimes, it's comfort in the form of His presence, holding us when we feel most broken. And sometimes, the answer doesn't come in the way we expect. Not everything requires an answer; some things simply require trust.

It's hardest to trust God when we feel lost and our hearts are crying out for answers. When we ask, *Why did this happen? Why is life so hard? Why did they have to go?* His response may not always satisfy us in the moment. But He reminds us to trust Him, to keep following Him, and to believe that He has a plan.

Grief can leave us feeling confused and overwhelmed, but God doesn't leave us in the dark to hurt us or confuse us. He works for our good, even when we don't understand. His answers may not come wrapped the way we want, but they always come.

Sometimes, God's answer to *why* is, *Trust me—I have a plan.* Other times, it's, *I gave life, and I know when it ends.* Or simply, *Look to me for strength, because your help comes from me.*

Sometimes we have questions for God not knowing what conversations our loved ones had with Him first.

It's okay to have questions. It's okay to ask, *Why?* But the most important thing is to trust the heart of God, knowing that He holds the answers, even when we don't understand.

Trusting His heart helps us understand His character. Again—grief is not a punishment. It's difficult because God orchestrated death to be a part of life. With death being the beginning of the beauty of eternity for the believer, it's a concept that will never fully make sense to the logical human brain—because for us, death is associated with loss and no return.

The way we lose people also provokes our questions. For me, it made me question why there was even a need for faith if it didn't heal my mother or my best friend. What's the reason if it didn't work in my favor?

One response I received was this: it forced me back to the feet of Jesus because I needed Him. And only through my faith could I believe that He was the remedy for this hurt.

Now—were these deaths meant to get my attention? Certainly not. But the aftermath provoked my questions in a really big way, creating space for necessary communication with God. Instead of answering all of my questions right away, God started depositing into me in a way that turned my pain into purpose—for people who had the same questions I had about grief.

Ask your questions. He does answer. The answer may not come wrapped the way we want it to, but oh, He does answer. God will not go silent on you while you cry. He will answer. He loves you that much. And so do I.

I love you.

Scripture: Proverbs 3:5-6 (AMP)

"Trust in and rely confidently on the Lord with all your heart and do not rely on your own insight or understanding. In all your ways know and acknowledge and recognize Him, And He will make your paths straight and smooth [removing obstacles that block your way."

Asking "why" is a natural part of grief. We want answers, closure, and understanding. But this scripture reminds us that trusting in God is more important than having all the answers. Our understanding is limited, but God sees the full picture. He knows what we cannot comprehend. When we lean on Him instead of our own reasoning, He promises to guide us. Even when life doesn't make sense, we can trust that God is leading us toward peace, healing, and purpose.

Affirmation:
"I may not understand everything, but I trust God's plan. His wisdom is greater than my questions, and His love for me is unshakable."

Final Thought:
You don't have to have all the answers to find peace. Trust that God's plan is still in motion, even when you don't see the full picture. His love is enough to carry you through.

REMEMBER THE LESSONS THEY TAUGHT YOU.

The lessons we learn from the people we love shape us into who we are. Every piece of advice, every skill, and every shared moment becomes a part of us. Whether they taught you how to tie your shoes, ride a bike, tell a joke, or enjoy a favorite show, those lessons live on in you.

Think about the deeper lessons they shared: how to handle your first heartbreak, how to face challenges, or how to take responsibility. Maybe they taught you about kindness, discipline, or managing money. These lessons have molded you into the person you are today and continue to guide your steps.

These teachings are more than memories—they're tools for living. They shape how we make decisions, how we care for others, and how we build our lives. The wisdom they passed on helps us face challenges, encourage others, and make bold choices.

Everything they taught you becomes a part of your daily life, from how you organize your day to how you show love to others. Even though they're no longer here, the lessons they left behind remain. They may not have taught us how to live without them, but their guidance gives us the strength to keep going.

These lessons are a gift. They teach us to love, have faith, believe in ourselves, and chase our dreams. Over time, you may notice how much their lessons make you more like them. What they shared with you wasn't just for the moment—it was meant to prepare you for the future.

Take time to remember these lessons and put them into practice. They weren't given to you by chance; they were meant to help you grow and live with purpose. Each lesson is a reminder that they're still a part of you, shaping you every day.

Even though they're gone, their lessons remain. They are

the blueprint for how to live, love, and move forward. These lessons remind us that, in so many ways, they're still with us.

They taught us what love was. How do I know? Because without them, we feel lost. The people in our lives—both those who've passed and those still present—are teaching us how to love. They teach us to love like there's no tomorrow while also hoping for the chance to love them again tomorrow.
They teach us to be gentle with people's hearts. From them, we've learned how to be a best friend and how to be a good person. We learn how to be someone others can count on—how to be dependable.

Grief teaches you to love. In all the hard emotions we face through it, grief teaches us how important it is to love, and to love fully. It shows us the areas where our love needs improvement, and it shows us the kind of love our heart really needs. Sometimes we don't experience this understanding until there's an absence.

The lessons come from what's now missing—the things we took for granted. Even the lessons they didn't mean to teach us still last. The conversations—good or bad—taught us what kind of communicators we are. The lessons are timeless and endless. They exist in everything we do because those lessons made room for our growth.

Teach the healthy things you've learned. And maybe unlearn some of the bad habits they unknowingly allowed from you.

Most of all, remember this lesson: You are loved!

I love you!

Scripture: Proverbs 4:7 (AMP)
"The beginning of wisdom is: Get [skillful and godly] wisdom [it is preeminent], And with all your acquiring, get understanding [actively seek spiritual discernment, mature comprehension, and logical interpretation]."

The lessons our loved ones teach us are not just random pieces of knowledge—they are wisdom meant to guide our lives. This scripture reminds us that wisdom is one of the most valuable things we can gain. The people we love impart wisdom through their words, actions, and even mistakes. These lessons shape us, give us direction, and help us make sound decisions. Though they may no longer be physically with us, their wisdom remains, offering guidance in every choice we make.

Affirmation:

"The lessons my loved one taught me will always be with me. Their wisdom lives in me, guiding my steps and shaping my future."

Final Thoughts:

Each lesson you carry is a gift, a reminder that your loved one's impact didn't end when they left this world. Their wisdom continues to live in you, influencing your decisions and shaping your journey. Honor them by living out what they taught you.

SADNESS IS ONLY TEMPORARY.

Sadness has not defeated you, even if it feels overwhelming at times. It hasn't taken over your life—it's just something that may feel bigger right now, but you are equipped to navigate through it. When I say sadness is temporary, it's not to diminish your right to grieve for as long as you need to. The Bible reminds us that weeping will turn into joy, and mourning will turn into dancing.

Your sadness doesn't have to exist alone. It can coexist with light, peace, and even happiness. Understanding that sadness is a natural part of grief—and that you don't control when it shows up—can help you take steps to manage it.

Being sad doesn't mean you can't laugh at a funny show or movie. It doesn't mean you can't spend time with people or fulfill your responsibilities. Sadness is temporary, but that doesn't mean it's tied to a specific timeline. Instead, it's tied to the control you give it.

You can feel sad and still be okay. You can feel sad and still have moments of joy. Sadness may come and go, but it doesn't last forever. It's an emotion, not something permanent.

Sadness is crying one minute after being happy. It's the reminder that you've experienced a loss. It's part of the process of grief, helping you accept what has happened. While sadness is temporary, it can still feel heavy.

Today, I encourage you to do your best not to let sadness weigh you down. Counter it with things that lift your spirits—spend time with loved ones, do something that makes you smile, or focus on what brings you peace. Sadness is a part of healing, but it doesn't have to define your journey.

While sadness is weighty, it does not have to stop you from flying. It's not meant to paralyze you. You can be sad and still have momentum. Don't let sadness take your focus. If you stop here, the side effects of sadness will grow. It will get so big that sadness is all you can see.

Don't let sadness and grief steal your vision. Push the best you can and as much as you can handle. Be gentle with yourself. Sadness is real—it exists where you wished there was joy. But joy is still present, even in your sadness. Welcome it. I know the emotions of the day seem overwhelming, but there is still light. Don't let sadness steal all the bases. There are still areas for happiness—embrace them.

The weight may never fully leave, but it will lighten. The heaviness is temporary, I promise.

I love you.

Scripture: Psalm 30:5 (NLT)
"Weeping may last through the night, but joy comes with the morning."

This verse reminds us that sadness, no matter how heavy, is not permanent. It acknowledges the reality of pain and grief but offers the reassurance that joy will come again. When we are in the middle of deep sorrow, it can feel endless, but God promises that we won't stay in that place forever. His comfort, peace, and even joy will return.

Sadness does not mean you are broken beyond repair. You are simply experiencing a natural part of loss. Your emotions may feel overwhelming, but they do not have the power to control you unless you let them. Lean into God's promise—pain is temporary, and healing will come in time.

Affirmation:
"I allow myself to feel sadness, but I will not let it define me. My joy is coming, and I trust God's promise to carry me through this season."

Final Thoughts:
Ask for grace as you grieve. Sadness is not a sign of weakness, and it does not mean you will never feel happiness again. Grief is a journey, not a destination. Keep moving forward, even if it's just one step at a time.

TEARS ARE NORMAL AND THEY ARE OK!

Our tears remind us that our emotions have a heart. In grief, tears often come without warning, making it hard to prepare for them. The tricky thing about tears is that they don't only appear when we're sad—they can come when we're angry, happy, overwhelmed, or even comforted. No matter the emotion, tears are proof that our feelings are real.

One moment, you may feel perfectly fine, and the next, you're crying. Once the tears come, they can be difficult to stop. Even happy tears can carry the weight of loss, reminding us of what is missing. Sad tears show the depth of our pain. Tears happen naturally, often without our control, and they are meant to be released.

Though tears may feel inconvenient, they serve a purpose. They help us process emotions, release pain, and heal. They are a sign of the love we've shared, the love we've received, and the love we still hold for the person we miss.

Crying can be frustrating because it forces us to pause and feel. Tears interrupt our schedules, making it hard to focus on anything else. But they are not something to be ashamed of—they are normal, and in fact, necessary. There is no way to avoid them, no quick fix to make them stop, no way to sleep them off. Tears are part of the grieving process, and the person we miss is worth every one of them.

Tears remind us that love doesn't disappear. They show that the people we have lost are still a part of us. They remind us of the joy, the memories, and the impact they had on our lives.

So don't see your tears as an inconvenience—embrace them. Let them flow alongside whatever emotions they bring. Tears are part of being human, a sign of how deeply we feel and love.

Don't be embarrassed by them. Don't hide them. Let them remind you that you have loved and been loved.

Tears are okay.

Tears are necessary. I know they make you feel weak, but they are a sign of strength. Crying—when you let it happen—is a sign that you are willing to submit to a needed pause to feel.

Tears are not a sign of weakness or even just pain leaving the body. If they were, I'm sure we'd all do it more often. Succumbing to your tears, especially as an adult, is admirable.

You don't have to hide your tears or cry in private. Exhale and cry when and where you need to. You don't need a special space or permission—all you have to do is be willing to give the tears the necessary time to flow.

Sure, you may want to stop them from happening, but you are not weak for allowing them. Tears are both normal and appropriate. Cry.

I love you.

Scripture: Psalm 56:8 (NLT)
"You keep track of all my sorrows. You have collected all my tears in your bottle. You have recorded each one in your book."

God sees every tear you cry, and not a single one goes unnoticed. Your grief is not ignored, dismissed, or forgotten—He holds your sorrow close, acknowledging your pain and standing beside you through it all. This verse reminds us that our emotions are valuable to God, and our tears are sacred.

Tears are not a sign of weakness; they are evidence of the depth of love you've experienced. Rather than seeing them as an inconvenience, allow them to be part of your healing.

Affirmation:
"My tears matter to God. They are not wasted, and neither is my pain. Each tear is a reflection of love, and I allow myself to feel, heal, and grow through them."

Final Thoughts:
Tears are not a sign of defeat; they are a sign that love remains. Let them come, knowing they are a step toward healing.

UNDERSTAND THAT THEIR ARE SAFE PEOPLE TO TALK TO. LET SOMEONE KNOW WHEN YOU'RE READY TO TALK.

Grief can make it hard to talk to people. Sometimes we shut down because we don't know how to express what we feel. Other times, we try to explain, but no one seems to understand. One of the hardest parts of grieving is feeling like no one truly gets what you're going through.

One thing grief teaches us is that no two people grieve the same way. Even if you and someone else lose the same person, your emotions will never be identical. For example, siblings who lose a parent may grieve differently because their relationships with that parent were different. Everyone experiences loss in their own way.

That's why it's so important to find someone safe to talk to. Talking about your grief makes your loss feel real—it helps put your emotions into words and process what you're feeling. A conversation with someone you trust can bring out emotions you didn't even realize were there, but that need to be released.

When looking for someone to talk to, choose wisely. Some people may not understand, and others may not care enough to try. But you need to talk about what you're experiencing, because if you don't face your emotions, you can't begin to process them. While grief can't be "solved," putting it into words helps you find some clarity. Talking about your anger, for example, can help you understand where it comes from and how to cope with it.

Grief doesn't come alone—it often piles on top of everything else you're going through, and sometimes, it feels like the breaking point. If you don't talk to someone, grief can consume you. Even if it feels easier to stay silent, find someone you can trust. This could be a therapist, a parent, a friend, a mentor, a teacher, or even a coworker—anyone who will listen and respond with care.

Journaling is helpful, and praying is powerful, but God also calls us to be in community. He doesn't want us to go through grief alone. You need someone who can talk back to you—someone who can offer words of comfort, truth, and support in a way your heart can receive.

These conversations won't always be easy. Sometimes, people may tell you things that are hard to hear. You may want to pull away. Don't. Keep talking. Keep expressing yourself. This is why safe spaces matter.

Grief can bring out emotions you didn't even know you had—some of them ugly, painful, or overwhelming. But opening up about them isn't about looking for someone to "fix" you; it's about being heard. The right person won't try to heal you, but they will listen to you.

Finding the right person to talk to may take time, but don't wait until you feel like you're drowning. Look for someone who notices when you need to talk, even when you don't say it out loud. Someone who understands your moods, your body language, and what you're going through.

Talking about grief isn't just about therapy—it's about expression. Grief can silence you if you let it. Don't let it. Speak up. Advocate for yourself. Find someone who will listen and help you release the weight you're carrying.

You don't have to go through this alone. Find your safe person and talk.

Utilize free professional resources as well. Find a safe resource. Sometimes talking to people you may not know can help you be more vulnerable in expression.

A grief coach or therapist is a good idea if you need it. Someone to help you with what you're feeling is good. Jesus plus a professional is a great recipe for help. Ask. I love you.

Scripture: Galatians 6:2 (NLT)

"Share each other's burdens, and in this way obey the law of Christ."

Grief was never meant to be carried alone. God designed us to be in community, to support one another, and to share our burdens. This verse reminds us that allowing others to walk with us through our pain is not a sign of weakness—it is a reflection of God's love in action.

Speaking about grief helps lighten the load. While no one can take your pain away completely, having someone listen, acknowledge your feelings, and offer support makes the weight of grief easier to bear. When you find a safe space to express yourself, healing becomes possible.

Affirmation:
"I do not have to grieve alone. I will allow myself to be supported, to speak, and to share my burdens with those who care about me."

Final Thought:
Grief can feel isolating, but you were never meant to go through it alone. Allow yourself to talk, to be heard, and to receive the support that God places in your life.

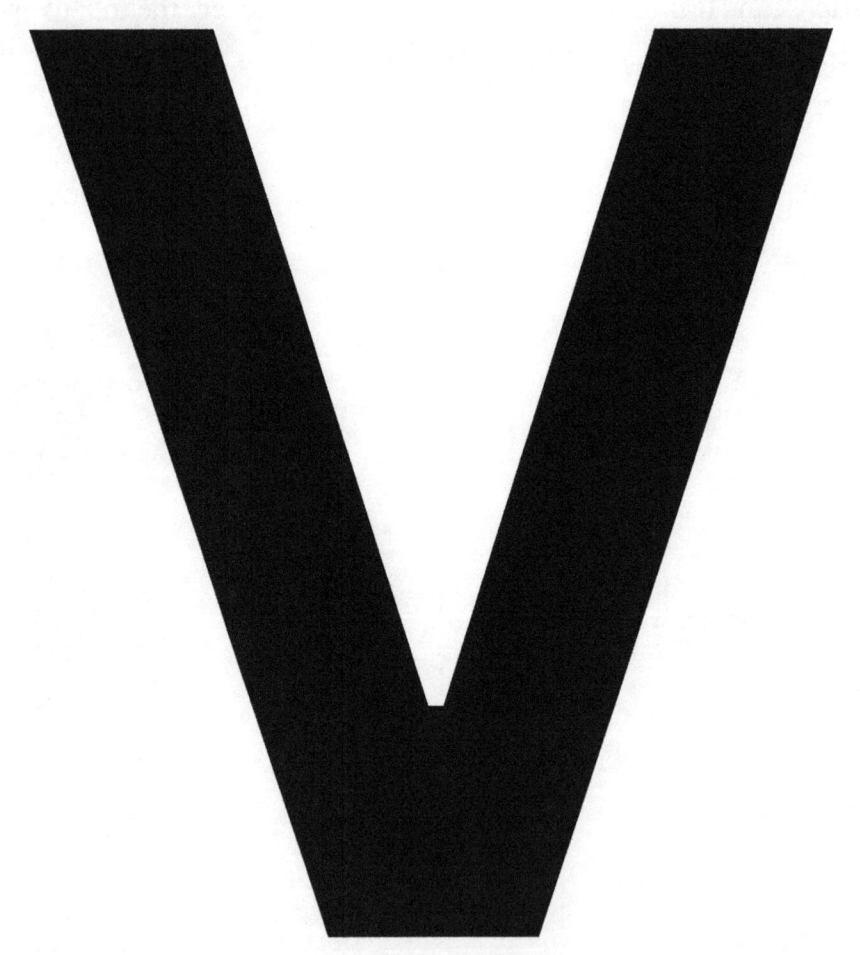

VISIT THE PLACES THAT MAKE YOU FEEL CLOSE TO THEM WHEN YOU NEED TO.

Going back to places you once shared with a loved one can be difficult. It's hard to visit a place that holds special memories, knowing they are no longer there with you. For some, this brings deep emotions that make it tough. For others, it can feel comforting, like a way to stay connected to them.

It's okay to visit places that remind you of your loved one—whether it's a cemetery, a favorite restaurant, a park, or any location where you spent time together. The key is to approach these visits in a way that brings comfort rather than deep sorrow.

When visiting, try to go with the mindset that they are still with you in spirit. Don't use these visits as moments to sink into grief, but as opportunities to feel close to them in a positive way. If visiting the cemetery, for example, go with a heart of love and remembrance rather than sadness. Bring flowers, say a few words, and then consider going somewhere that brings good memories.

One helpful tip is to set a time limit when visiting certain places, especially cemeteries. Staying too long can sometimes intensify grief, making it harder to leave. Instead, keep the visit brief, then do something uplifting—like going to your favorite spot together or treating yourself to something they enjoyed. This helps balance the sadness with happy memories.

It's also okay to revisit places that brought you joy together—whether it's a church, a concert venue, a movie theater, or even a park. The first time will be the hardest, but if you find comfort in it, it's okay to make it a habit. Just be mindful that it stays healthy, doesn't affect your well-being, and doesn't put financial strain on you.

If done with the right mindset, visiting familiar places can be a beautiful way to honor their memory. However, if it leads to dwelling only on the moment they were lost, it can become unhealthy. Instead, find creative ways to make these places feel familiar again—ways that bring back the joy, not just the loss.

Your loved one would want you to continue enjoying the things that made you happy. Don't stop doing what brings you joy. Keep living, keep making memories, and most importantly, allow yourself to have happy moments—not just for them, but for you. You deserve to experience joy.

Be careful, as best you can, to not site-associate too much, because you will deprive yourself of good places.

On the other hand, if certain places become too difficult to visit often—like the cemetery—either don't go or only visit on special occasions and anniversaries. Please don't attach this to you "leaving them alone," not loving them, or being made to forget them. That's not the case.

You must use wisdom and do what's best for your mental health. One way to judge whether or not you can handle it is by checking how long it takes you to recover after going, and what your ability to leave looks like.

I know it may be difficult, but there are still ways to honor them. Find creative, safe ways to do so. Visit these places with the intention to find at least one reason to smile!

There may be some places where these overwhelming feelings can't be avoided. Use your discernment—you know what you can handle.

Be mindful not to neglect those grieving with you at these places and events. God will equip you. Show up, embrace your emotions, and be supportive there. There will be peace there

for you. Welcome it.
    I love you.

Scripture: Isaiah 41:10 (NLT)
"Don't be afraid, for I am with you. Don't be discouraged, for I am your God. I will strengthen you and help you. I will hold you up with my victorious right hand."

Grief can make us feel vulnerable, especially when visiting places that hold strong memories. But this verse reminds us that God is always with us. You are not alone when you step into those familiar spaces—God's presence strengthens you and helps you find peace.

It's okay to revisit meaningful places, but don't let them become places of deep sorrow. Instead, let them remind you of the joy, love, and good memories you shared. Even when grief feels heavy, God holds you up, helping you navigate through your emotions with strength.

Affirmation:
"I am not alone in my grief. God strengthens me, holds me up, and helps me find comfort in my memories."

Final Thought:
Revisiting familiar places can bring both sadness and healing. Allow yourself to feel, but don't let the sadness consume you. Instead, find joy in the memories, knowing your loved one would want you to continue living with hope.

WAKING UP IN A GOOD MOOD MAY BE DIFFICULT SOME DAYS BUT KEEP SHOWING UP; THE BEST WAY YOU KNOW HOW.

Waking up is always a toss-up! You never know which side of the bed you're going to wake up on. You never know how hot or cold the pillow is going to be to judge the temperature of how your day is going to look. The most important thing is that you get up, even if you feel that you can't rise to the occasion every day. Find ways to show up for yourself. Find ways to still show up for the people you love. The demand from them will absolutely look different depending on how you can show up, but try your best.

There are many days when waking up may feel like you are physically carrying a ton of bricks and can't move. There will be days when the emotions tied to "getting up" consume you because so much is weighing you down. Push through as best you can. The biggest thing to realize is that in the places you can't show up, God is still there and will always perform on your behalf. All you have to do is stand; and in this case, standing is getting up.

Be wise and be healthy as well because there may be days when you need to rest. Don't overwork yourself to the point where you work yourself into a frenzy, become overstimulated, and feel unsure of what to do next. Don't use getting up as a reason to mask your emotions. The hardest part of waking up is understanding how important it is to not wake up with the intention to mask, and in the same breath, it's important to understand not to wake up with a knife. Don't mask how you're feeling, but don't allow how you're feeling to cut others during your day. Ask for the peace that you need.

How you wake up matters. One of the best ways to command and control exactly how you wake up is by waking up and commanding your day. Wake up saying, "Even though I'm going through what I'm going through, I'm going to have a good day." "My mind is going to be sound." "My heart is going to love." "My spirit is going to be lifted." "Something is going to happen today to make me smile."

Find things to look forward to in waking up. Make sure to spend time with those you love, but set aside time to spend with yourself to sit with your feelings. Don't make waking up burdensome. I know what it can feel like to wake up and feel like there are so many things that you have to get to that are demanding and required of you—like work, school, and other tasks—but don't be consumed by the projects of the day to the point that you forget that you are your project. You are what's important right now.

How you wake up matters. How you step out of bed matters. How you command your day matters. How you show up for yourself matters. How you deal with your emotions minute by minute, second by second matters. What you allow to consume you matters. Be intentional about the things that bring you joy, things you can look forward to when you wake up.

This is so important because waking up is something that not everyone gets the opportunity to do. Grief teaches us that every day is a gift. Every day is a present. Every day is a blessing. Don't let grief jip you out of the opportunity to live. Every day you wake up, there is purpose. Every day you wake up, is a gift. Every day you wake up, there is a task that is going to better you, and it's going to also change someone's life because you chose to rise. Shine as best as you can. Remember to take it easy on yourself. Be patient with yourself. Know that this is new. Feel the feelings that you feel when you wake up and then command them. Speak things that are not as though they are.

Start your day with prayer. Start your day with communication with people that you love. Start your day with things that will make you smile and laugh. Start your day with music that will uplift you. Start your day commanding and controlling grief, letting it know that it does not have control over you.

Wake up, show up the best you can.

What you can't handle, God already has a grip on. Just show up and put one foot in front of the other.

This is how we'll make it through our days.

I love You.

Scripture: Lamentations 3:22-23 (ESV)
"The steadfast love of the Lord never ceases; his mercies never come to an end; they are new every morning; great is your faithfulness."

No matter what yesterday looked like, today is a new day with new mercies. Every morning, God gives us another chance to rise, to live, and to embrace the gift of life. Even in grief, His love remains, His strength is available, and His faithfulness is constant.

Waking up doesn't mean you have to feel completely okay—but it does mean that God has given you another opportunity to experience His grace. When the weight of grief makes it hard to start your day, remember that you don't have to do it alone. God is holding you up, and His mercies are always fresh.

Affirmation:
"I am covered by God's new mercies every morning. Even when grief feels heavy, I have the strength to rise and embrace the day with purpose."

Final Thought:
Each morning is an invitation to experience God's faithfulness. Take it one step at a time, knowing that you are not alone. Your presence in this world still matters, and there is a purpose for your day—even in the smallest moments.

X-RAY MAY SHOW THAT YOUR HEART IS BROKEN BUT IT WILL SMILE AGAIN.

Your heart is not shattered beyond repair. Grief has a way of making us believe that heartbreak means we must die too. But I'm here to encourage you today—it is possible to live through this heartbreak. There is still life, not just on the other side of this heartbreak, but even through it.

Lately, I've been asking myself: If someone were to take an X-ray of my heart, what exactly would they see? I had to remind myself that, despite everything I'm feeling and going through—grief, depression, anger, hurt, even hatred—all of these emotions are real and raw, but they do not define me. I had to understand that if someone looked at my heart, the things that make me me still exist.

Don't let grief overpower your essence. When someone looks at your heart, they should still see you. It's okay for people to see what grief has attached to you. It's okay for them to see the emotions. It's okay for them to see that your heart is broken. It's even okay if they see moments of defeat. But don't ever let grief change your heart.

Don't let losing someone change how you love the people who are still here. Don't let losing someone take away your compassion. Don't let grief make you believe that you are not worthy of love.

You are worthy. You are necessary. You are so loved. You still matter.

Even in pain, you have purpose. Even through tears, you still have a calling. You inspire so many people every day. When people look at your heart, they still see:

- A person of compassion.
- A person of light.
- A person of love.
- A person who gives.

Don't let grief change that.

Grief is like a weed—it tries to take root and choke out the things that make you you. But don't let it. Don't give it that power. Be mindful and intentional about protecting your heart, not just in how others see you, but in how you see yourself.

Remind yourself of what exists inside your heart. If you start to feel like parts of you are slipping away, remind yourself of what should be there.

- You are still strong.
- You are still capable.
- You still matter.
- You are still a life-changer.
- You are still a warrior.
- You are a survivor.

As broken as your heart may feel—whether today, tomorrow, or years from now—remember this: healing is not about stitching up the hole that grief left behind.

Losing someone creates a void that can never truly close. Grief is about learning to adapt, not learning how to erase the hole. If you spend your time trying to seal it, you will drown in the effort. Instead, plant flowers where the hole is, so something beautiful can bloom from it.

Don't try to close the hole. It's okay if there is still an empty space on the X-ray of your heart. Just make sure weeds aren't growing there.

Don't let bitterness take root.

Don't let hatred or hurt grow.

Don't let envy and anger fester.

Fill the void with beauty. Talk to God about what your heart needs. Allow Him to plant new seeds.

If someone were to take an X-ray of your heart today, no matter how imperfect it may look, let there still be beauty inside it. Because those beautiful things will ensure that one day, your heart will smile again.

I love You.

Scripture: Psalm 147:3 (HCSB)
"He heals the brokenhearted and binds up their wounds."

Grief can make us feel like our hearts are beyond repair. The pain can feel so overwhelming that it seems impossible to heal. But this verse reminds us that God is in the business of healing broken hearts. He doesn't just leave us to figure out how to cope—He actively works to mend the wounds that grief leaves behind.

Healing doesn't mean forgetting. It doesn't mean the pain vanishes overnight. But it does mean that over time, God can restore your heart, piece by piece. You don't have to rush the process, and you don't have to heal alone. Trust that even in the deepest hurt, God is working to make your heart whole again.

Affirmation:
"My heart is healing. I am not broken beyond repair. God is binding up my wounds and making me whole again."

Final Thought:
Healing through grief is a journey, not a destination. You don't have to "get over it"—you just have to keep moving forward. Let God fill the empty spaces in your heart with love, peace, and purpose.

YOU ARE NOT TO BLAME AND GOD DID NOT IGNORE YOUR PRAYERS. HE SIMPLY HAD OTHER PLANS.

Loss is not a punishment. God is not trying to punish you, and He does not hate you.

One of the hardest things to explain in grief—to others and to our own hearts—is that what is happening to us is not a punishment for something we have done. This is especially true when we lose someone suddenly, without warning. It's easy to blame ourselves, to feel like we didn't pray hard enough, or that if we had just done something differently, the outcome would have changed.

When you have prayed, fasted, and interceded for someone's healing, only for them to still pass away, it can feel like your prayers weren't working. But God has not stopped hearing you.

It is difficult to understand how much higher His plans are, how much broader His thoughts are, and how strategic He is. These things are not easy to grasp because, in grief, all we can think about is how deeply we are affected. The way we lose someone often shapes how we process and feel that loss.

The Bible tells us that when we grieve, we do not grieve like the world—we grieve with hope. And the reason we grieve with hope is because God still has plans for us. He still loves us. He still cares for us. He is still mindful of us. He still has a purpose for our lives.

Grieving with hope requires us to continue believing in Him. It requires us to remain in prayer, to stay connected to Him, and to hold on to faith—even when our faith is shaken. It requires us to trust that He is still Lord over our lives. Grieving with hope allows us to grieve with the promise that one day, we will see our loved one again.

None of this is your fault.

None of this is your fault.

None of this is your fault.

God loves us so much that even through loss, He surrounds us with people who still love us. While they can never replace the person we lost, He loves us enough to not leave us alone. He places people in our lives who understand our hearts, who uplift our spirits, who cover us in prayer, and who help us navigate these hard times.

He loves us enough to surround us with people who will support us, guide us, and be there when we need them. He loves us enough to provide tangible, loving people for us to lean on.

I know you're hurting. I know you may feel like you are to blame.

The hardest truth to accept is that this had nothing to do with you.

God's plans are higher. They are different, and they are not always what we assume they should be—because we do not think like Him. Losing people is one of the hardest things we face, because we don't get them back. But we do have a promise that we will see them again if we live according to God's word.

Don't grow weary.

Don't lose your hope.

Be hopeful. Be steadfast. Be unmovable. Keep walking in faith—even while grieving.

Understand that His ways are not your ways, and His thoughts are not your thoughts.

Before you were even born, He knew you. He had a plan for you—to give you a future and a hope.

Don't let blame, guilt, shame, or hurt convince you that you don't deserve to live. Don't let grief consume you. I know this season feels dark. I know you may feel lost.

But none of this is your fault.

As easy as it is to blame God for what has happened, try a different approach. Let Him guide you. He still has the answers.

He is still the answer. He still answers prayers.

Don't be deceived.

I love You.

Scripture: Romans 8:28 (AMP)

"And we know [with great confidence] that God [who is deeply concerned about us] causes all things to work together [as a plan] for good for those who love God, to those who are called according to His plan and purpose."

When we lose someone, we love, it can feel like a punishment—like God is taking from us for reasons we can't understand. This verse reminds us that God is always working things together for our good, even when we can't see it. That doesn't mean loss isn't painful or that we won't struggle to understand why it happened, but it does mean that God's plan is bigger than what we can see right now.

Instead of seeing grief as a punishment, we can choose to trust that God is still moving, still caring for us, and still making a way for healing. Even in pain, His plan is still for our good.

Affirmation:
"God is not punishing me. He is still with me, still working for my good, and still loving me through this pain."

Final Thought:
Grief can make you feel abandoned, but you are not alone. God is walking with you through this, and in time, He will bring purpose even from your pain.

ZEPHANIAH 3:17 SAYS THE LORD IS IN THE MIDST HE IS SO PRESENT. DON'T YOU EVER FORGET THAT YOU ARE LOVED AND YOU ARE NEVER ALONE.

Even in loss, we have not lost God, and He has not lost you. As cloudy as it may seem, as hard as it may be, and as alone as you may feel, God has not left you. He has not forsaken you, and His promise to never leave or forsake you has not become null and void simply because you are experiencing loss.

You are never alone. You will never be alone. He's not going anywhere.

This is an important time—when your faith may be shaken, and when it may feel impossible to pray because you don't even know what to pray for. Even when it feels like He is far away, don't forget to lean on Him. As difficult as that may seem, try your best to do it.

Even when He feels distant, He is still singing over you. He is still covering you, still interceding for you. In this confusing time, when it feels like you can't feel Him, see Him, or hear Him, know that He is still speaking and loving you deeply.

He does not leave us just because we lose someone we love.

- He is still our Comforter.
- He is still our ever-present help.
- He is still love.
- He is still joy.
- He is still peace.
- He is still kind.
- He still understands, even when we don't.

While we may not understand why this is happening, He understands exactly what our hearts are feeling. It's easy to blame Him because we know everything is in His control. But trust that what He allows is never for your harm.

Loss hurts. Grief is difficult. But it is not for our destruction.

When we lose people, the goal is not for us to lose ourselves.

I know exactly what it feels like to feel lost in grief. But don't let it consume you. Pull yourself up in the best way you can. Allow others to lift you when you need it. Let them build you up.

But most importantly, never, ever believe that God has removed His hand from you.

- Never believe He has taken His arms from around you.
- Never believe He has taken His hand off your life.

He is still good.

He is still God.

He is still faithful.

I know it hurts. I know you don't understand. I know this is confusing, and I know you feel like He owes you answers. But remember how faithful He still is. Remember how much He has loved you. And know that He is still concerned about the things that concern you.

He loves you.

He loves you so much that He is still mighty to save you, deliver you, and rejoice over you.

Don't let grief be the reason you stop communing with Him.

Even if you can't hear what He wants to say right now, He still has a plan. He still has a purpose.

Don't let grief detach you from your source.

God loves you deeply, and we are going to get through this together. I know it's hard. I know it's painful.

Even though He allowed it, He will still see you through it.

That is His promise.

He will never leave you. There is nothing you can do to make Him leave.

- You can't out-sin His love.

- You can't push Him away.
- He will always be drawing you back.

Don't let grief detach you from Him. Stay connected.

We will never have to grieve God—because with Him, death does not exist. With Him, there is only life—full life, complete life, and life abundantly.

He desires for you to have that, even in the midst of your pain.

Stay connected to Him. He will forever be present.

I love You.

Scripture: Zephaniah 3:17(NIV)

"The Lord your God is with you, He is mighty to save. He will take great delight in you; He will quiet you with His love; He will rejoice over you with singing."

When grief tries to convince us that we are forgotten or unworthy of joy, this verse stands as a gentle yet powerful reminder: God is not only present—He is active. He is mighty enough to heal, save, and deliver, even in our most broken places.

He sees your pain, and yet He delights in you. That may feel hard to grasp when sorrow is heavy, but God's love doesn't shift based on our emotions. His song over you is not silenced by your sadness. His strength is not weakened by your tears. Even when you feel undone, He is restoring you. Even when you feel shattered, He is healing you. God doesn't just sit beside you quietly—He rejoices over you with singing, declaring that you are still His, still loved, and still worthy of hope.

Let His love quiet your heart today. Let His presence remind you that healing is possible, joy is still coming, and you are never alone.

Affirmation:

"God is with me. He delights in me, sings over me, and holds me through every wave of grief."

Final Thought:

You are not forgotten in your sorrow. God is not silent in your sadness. He is with you—strong enough to save, gentle enough to comfort, and loving enough to sing over you while you heal. Even in the quiet moments of grief, His presence is steady and His love is still loud.

A Gift That Lasts Forever

It is my sincerest prayer that this book has blessed you beyond measure. It's not my intention for this to be a one-time read, but something you can return to whenever you need it. Mark your favorite pages, take notes, and pray over yourself daily.

As we come to the close of this book, I want to leave you with the greatest gift of all: the gift of salvation through Jesus Christ. It is impossible to truly grieve with hope without Jesus living in your heart. To experience the fullness of His peace and sufficiency, you must first accept Him as Lord of your life. He loves you deeply and chooses you every single day.

You can welcome Him into your heart by following these four simple steps:

- A: Acknowledge that you need a Savior—Jesus Christ.
- B: Believe in your heart that Jesus was born, lived, and died on the cross for you and your sins.
- C: Confess with your mouth that He is coming back for you.
- D: Declare that He is Lord of your life.

If you are already a believer, I encourage you to cling closer and tighter to Christ. He is going to reveal Himself and His closeness to you in ways you can't even imagine. Be reminded that grief is not something you are battling alone—because God is fighting for you! All you have to do is stand. He won't let you fall. Cleave to Him. His grace is still sufficient for you! You are not abandoned. You are not being punished. Do your best to smile when you can, and let your living be intentional.

Let's pray together:

Lord, I come to You right now on behalf of the person reading this. God, I ask that You meet them right here, right now—exactly where they are. Let them feel Your love and experience the power of Your presence. Cover them in Your peace.

Lord, we do not blame You. Forgive us for harboring that emotion against you, due to our anger, lack of understanding and hurt.

I pray in the name of Jesus, as they welcome You into their heart, that You begin to take full charge of their life. May they find true rest and hope in You. As they journey through grief, remind them daily that You are near. Help us to keep our minds stayed on You, so You will keep us in perfect peace.

We know we can do all things through You because You give us strength. We reject fear, because You have not given us a spirit of fear, but of power, love, and a sound mind. We trust You, Lord—with our lives, our pain, and even our shortcomings.

Help us to lean not on our own understanding, but to rest in You. Thank You for being our constant, for never leaving or forsaking us. Thank You for being near to the brokenhearted, for binding up our wounds, for collecting every tear, and for singing over us.

We acknowledge You as our Keeper, our Healer, our Hope, and our Peace. Thank You for Your sovereignty and Your control. I love You with my whole heart. Thank You for saving me and thank you for grieving with me. In Jesus' name, I pray—Amen.

The Romans Road to Salvation (Scripture Path):

- Romans 3:23 (NLT)

"For everyone has sinned; we all fall short of God's glorious standard."

- Romans 6:23 (HCSB)

"For the wages of sin is death, but the gift of God is eternal life in Christ Jesus our Lord."

- Romans 5:8 (AMP)

"But God clearly shows and proves His own love for us by the fact that while we were still sinners, Christ died for us."

- Romans 10:9 (ESV)

"If you confess with your mouth that Jesus is Lord and believe in your heart that God raised him from the dead, you will be saved."

- Romans 10:13 (NLT)

"For everyone who calls on the name of the Lord will be saved."

You are loved. You are seen. You are never alone.

Hold on to that truth—and keep walking with hope.

So… you said the prayer. You opened your heart. You made room for healing.

That's big. That's beautiful. That's bold.

Now what?

1. **Get connected to a community.**

Grief can feel isolating, but healing happens in community.

Start looking for a Bible-believing church near you—a place that teaches God's Word, makes space for real-life struggles, and encourages growth in your faith.

You don't have to do life (or grief) alone. There are people out there ready to walk with you, pray with you, and pour into you. Let them.

Not sure where to start? Look online for churches in your area, visit a few, and ask God to lead you to the right one. And when you find it—get involved.

2. **Read the Word (even a little at a time).**

The Bible isn't just a book—it's life, strength, and peace.

If you're new to reading scripture, start with the book of John or Psalms.

Read a little each day. Let God speak back to you. Highlight verses that bring you peace, and go back to them when things feel heavy.

Start simple. Start small. But just start.

3. **Talk to God—often.**

Prayer doesn't have to sound perfect. It doesn't need big words or fancy structure.

Talk to God like you'd talk to someone who really, really loves you—because He does.

Tell Him how you feel. Ask Him for help. Thank Him for what He's done. And listen. His voice may come through peace, scripture, or the quiet reassurance in your heart.

4. Journal your journey.

Use a notebook, your phone, or the pages in this book. Write how you're feeling. Write the scriptures that stick with you. Write what God shows you.

This isn't just for memories—it's for progress.

You'll be surprised what healing looks like when you can look back and see how far you've come.

5. Give yourself grace.

Healing isn't instant. Growth isn't linear.

Some days will feel better than others. That's okay.

God is not looking for perfection—He's just looking for your heart.

Keep showing up. Keep trusting. Keep breathing. One day at a time.

6. Remember the promise.

You are not alone.

You are not forgotten.

You are not too broken to be restored.

"The Lord is close to the brokenhearted and saves those who are crushed in spirit." — Psalm 34:18 (NLT)

This is just the beginning. There's so much more ahead of you.

You are still here—and that means your story isn't over.

WHAT HAS THIS BOOK TAUGHT YOU?

AFTER READING THIS BOOK, WHAT CAN YOU TEACH OTHERS?

WHAT QUESTIONS DO YOU HAVE?

PRAYER REQUESTS

WHAT ARE SOME NEW THINGS YOU ARE WILLING TO TRY?

WHO ARE SOME SAFE PEOPLE YOU CAN EXPRESS YOURSELF TO?

www.ingramcontent.com/pod-product-compliance
Lightning Source LLC
Chambersburg PA
CBHW021156160426
43194CB00007B/765